Reason and Reality in the Methodologies of Economics

To Herb Driver

My first guide to the fascinating terrain that lies between economics and philosophy.

Reason and Reality in the Methodologies of Economics

An Introduction

Glenn Fox
Professor of Agricultural Economics,
University of Guelph, Canada

ADVANCES IN ECONOMIC METHODOLOGY

Edward Elgar
Cheltenham, UK • Lyme, US

Published by
Edward Elgar Publishing Limited
8 Lansdown Place
Cheltenham
Glos GL50 2HU
UK

Edward Elgar Publishing, Inc.
1 Pinnacle Hill Road
Lyme
NH 03768
US

A catalogue record for this book
is available from the British Library

Library of Congress Cataloguing in Publication Data
Fox, Glenn.
    Reason and reality in the methodologies of economics : an
introduction / Glenn Fox.
    (Advances in economic methodology)
    Includes bibliographical references.
    1. Economics—Methodology—History—20th century.   I. Title.
II. Series
HB131.F69   1997
330'.072—dc21   97–5356
                                                                          CIP
ISBN 1 85898 597 8   *1966179*

Printed and bound in Great Britain by
Hartnolls Limited, Bodmin, Cornwall

Contents

Figures

Tables

Preface

This book examines the scientific credentials of economics. It is concerned with what economists have written about the process of theory appraisal. An anonymous reviewer observed that I take the methodological writings of economists about economics as my reference point and place less emphasis on the application of the doctrines of general methodologists of science to economics than has typically been done by other writers in this field. My thesis is that economists have had quite a lot to say about the rules for theory appraisal in their discipline. There are at least five major schools of thought on the subject: positivism, instrumentalism, *a priorism*, realism and rhetorical analysis. Rare skirmishes between schools have generated much heat but little light regarding the fundamental differences between the contending positions. One of the aims of this book is to outline the foundational ideas behind each of the five major positions on the philosophy of science that have been advocated by economists. I also assess the extent to which economists have abided by their methodological doctrines.

Although the study of methodology continues to be under-represented in curricula of economics and related disciplines, methodological writings by economists and about economics are experiencing a renaissance. Some writers have suggested that economics is in the midst of a crisis. The dimensions of this alleged crisis are measured in charges of excessive formalism, loss of relevance, inappropriate pedagogy, and questionable or at least not very robust empirical results. Economists and philosophers of science are once again asking if economics needs a separate set of rules for theory appraisal, different from those used in the natural sciences. But the perception that a crisis is at hand is not the only or the best argument for the study of methodology. The most compelling reason for economists to take methodology seriously is that it is a necessary prerequisite for critical thought in any scientific discipline. Critical thinking needs to appreciate the limits of knowledge. It needs to understand the underlying causes of controversies in a field of study. It needs to know the purpose or purposes of inquiry in a discipline. It needs to know the sources from which knowledge claims are produced in a discipline. These are all methodological questions.

McCloskey (1990) claims that 'The methodological thinking of economists is a scandal'. He bases this indictment on his assessment that economists have not kept up with recent developments in the philosophy of science. Therefore they are trying to live up to a set of scientific criteria that have been abandoned. This book does not attempt to explore recent developments within the philosophy of science as much as it attempts to help economists listen to one another on matters methodological. I am convinced that resolution of existing and emerging methodological controversies in economics must begin with a better understanding of the various voices within the discipline.

Glenn Fox
University of Guelph

1. Is There a Crisis in Economics?

In the less philosophically-minded Anglo-Saxon countries it is hardly surprising that many have turned their backs in impatience on 'this noisy conflict of half-truths angrily denying one another', and have abandoned the interminable wranglings and controversies of the 'methodologists' and 'philosophers' for seemingly more constructive work. But this evasion can only be temporary. For it can be fairly insisted that no advance in the elegance and comprehensiveness of the theoretical superstructure can make up for the vague and uncritical formulation of the basic concepts and postulates, and sooner or later – and at the moment it seems to be sooner – attention will have to return to the foundations.

(Terence Hutchison, 1938/1960, p. 5)

The question posed in the title of this chapter may seem peculiar to many students of economics. Don't government agencies and private firms continue to seek the advice of economists on a wide range of issues? Aren't economists' ideas beginning to influence policy actions in such diverse arenas as welfare reform and environmental protection? Isn't a Nobel Prize awarded annually to a recognized contributor to economic science? And yet murmurs of dissent are becoming increasingly audible in the home of *homo economicus*.

External critics of economics are not new. The Austrian economist Ludwig von Mises claimed that criticism from without was an inevitable consequence of economic inquiry, given the constraints on political action that are often illuminated by economic analysis. Expressions such as 'There's no such thing as a free lunch' have nothing to do with mid-day dining and everything to do with debunking political schemes that promise to deliver benefits to voters without any cost to anyone. Sir Karl Popper (1989, pp. 342–3) has described the function of economics as the articulation of rules stating what cannot be achieved through political means. For example, 'You cannot, without increasing productivity, raise the real income of the working population' or 'You cannot equalize real incomes and at the same time raise productivity'.

One contribution of economics is to remind us that if a policy proposal sounds too good to be true, it probably is. People with a less sceptical perception of the political process, or those who aspire to use that process to advance their own ends, would naturally object to economists' pronouncements that indicate limitations on the scope of political action. The eighteenth century French economist Frederick Bastiat, who was also a parliamentarian and journalist, frequently identified the political motivation behind those who objected to the application of the principles of economics.

1

But more recently, criticism from within the ranks of practising economists has become more frequent and more troubling. Many of these critics question the usefulness of theorizing in economics as it is currently practised. Others have suggested that the purpose of the discipline has deviated from its historical and correct focus. These are fundamental methodological issues. Unfortunately, the study of methodology has not been high on the list of economists' priorities for several generations. As a result, we are often ill prepared to discuss the field without our conversation degenerating into familiar but threadbare clichés. It is encouraging, however, that once again, economists are examining the foundations of their subject. The ranks of the economist–philosophers and of the philosopher–economists have been growing since the 1970s. Books, articles and conference proceedings on methodological subjects are becoming more common (see Table 1.1).

Methodology is concerned about theory appraisal. It is concerned with how economists should and how economists do choose among alternative theories of human social interaction. Philosophers of science have produced several theories of theory appraisal, or methodologies. The thesis of this book is that economists employ several methodologies. Usually, economists select elements from different philosophical positions in an eclectic or pragmatic fashion. On occasion, an economist will advocate a pure form of a methodological position, but this is rare. This practice has led to fragmentation and confusion in the way that economists discuss issues related to theory appraisal. Competing methodological doctrines are often incompatible, at least on some dimensions.

Economists are increasingly divided on some very basic methodological questions. The almost monolithic consensus on the purpose of economic inquiry, which has prevailed from the publication of Lionel Robbins's influential essay in 1932, is unravelling. Economists also disagree on the status of different sources of knowledge about economic phenomena and on the role of knowledge from different sources in the evaluation of theories. To a lesser extent, controversies with regard to the appropriate structure of economic theories, and the scope of application of economic knowledge are emerging. But the study of methodology has occupied a backwater in the pedagogy of economics and agricultural economics for several generations. Most economists learned what they know about theory appraisal through casual remarks in classrooms and from perfunctory discussions in introductory chapters of textbooks. Since the philosophy of science is not taken seriously in the education of most economists, they are often unaware of the origins of many of the issues that divide their discipline.

Table 1.1   Recent contributions to economic methodology

Books
1975   Hollis and Nell, *Rational Economic Man*
1976   Rosenberg, *Microeconomic Laws: A Philosophical Analysis*
1978   Hutchison, *On Revolutions and Progress in Economic Knowledge*
1979   Stewart, *Reasoning and Method in Economics*
1980   Blaug, *The Methodology of Economics*
1981   Hutchison, *The Politics and Philosophy of Economics*
1982   Caldwell, *Beyond Positivism: Economic Methodology in the Twentieth Century*
       Boland, *The Foundations of Economic Method*
1985   McCloskey, *The Rhetoric of Economics*
1988   Phelby, *Methodology and Economics*
1989   Roy, *Philosophy of Economics: On the Scope of Reason in Economic Inquiry*
       Boland, *The Methodology of Economic Model Building*
1990   McCloskey, *If You're So Smart: The Narrative of Economic Expertise*
1991   Hamouda and Price, *Verification in Economics and History*
       Redman, *Economics and the Philosophy of Science*
1992   Hausman, *The Inexact and Separate Science of Economics*
       Blaug, *The Methodology of Economics* (Second edition)
       Rosenberg, *Economics − Mathematical Politics or the Science of Diminishing Returns*

Collections of Essays
1976   Latsis (ed.), *Method and Appraisal in Economics*
1978   Machlup, *Methodology of Economics and Other Social Sciences*
1979   Buchanan, *What Should Economists Do?*
1980   Samuels (ed.), *The Methodology of Economic Thought*
1981   Pitt (ed.), *Philosophy in Economics*
1983   *Methodological Controversy in Economics: Historical Essays in Honour of T.W. Hutchison*
1984   Hausman (ed.), *The Philosophy of Economics: An Anthology*
       Caldwell (ed.), *Appraisal and Criticism in Economics*
1988   de Marchi (ed.), *The Popperian Legacy in Economics*
       Klamer, McCloskey and Solow (eds), *The Consequences of Economic Rhetoric*

LISTENING TO THE CRITICS WITHIN

Doubts about the state of economic theory are being voiced by economists with increasing frequency. The remainder of this chapter examines some of the leading areas of dissent. To most economists, being scientific has something to do with testing models and theories against facts. This makes the criticism of economists such as Edward Leamer and Wassily Leontief and the findings of the *Journal of Money, Credit and Banking* study (Dewald *et al.*, 1986), so troubling. A second area of doubt involves the way in which economics is taught, particularly at the graduate level. Recent surveys of faculty, graduate students and employers have revealed worrying trends in the pedagogy of economics. One of these trends, the shift from policy relevance to formalism, extends to more than just the teaching enterprise. Several prominent economists have lamented a shift away from policy relevance in academic research.

THE RELATIONSHIP BETWEEN THEORY AND DATA

> I doubt ... that traditional econometric methods will survive.
>
> (Fischer Black, 1982, p. 35)

There is an unmistakable atmosphere of scepticism about the state of empirical work in economics. It is widely, if not always publicly, admitted by economists that empirical economic models have performed poorly in predicting major economic events. The oil price increases of the early 1970s, the co-existence of high inflation and high unemployment that followed and numerous dramatic downturns in important stock markets continue to be a source of embarrassment. Added to this record are the apparent fragility of statistical inferences derived from econometric models; apparently small variations in model structure or data can produce dramatic differences in parameter values, and a weak track record in replication of the results of other researchers.

Weakness of the empirical foundations of economics is a recurring theme among critics from within. There are several dimensions to this criticism. To some writers, the problem lies with an inordinate emphasis on the development of theories and techniques, on the study of hypothetical worlds that may not exist, at the expense of careful observation of phenomena in the world that we know does exist. Critical scholarship on the state of econometric practice, as exemplified by Chris Sims's (1980) 'Macroeconomics and Reality', David Hendry's (1980) 'Econometrics – Alchemy or Science?' and Edward Leamer's (1983) 'Let's Take the Con out of Econometrics', cast a shadow on the reputation of empirical research. The findings of the *Journal of Money, Credit and Banking* study reported by Dewald *et al.* (1986) indicate serious problems in the replication of published empirical results. And Mark Blaug's (1980/1992) conclusion that economists are reluctant to expose their theories to the possibility of contradiction by data does not inspire confidence. Wassily Leontief and Ronald Coase have criticized contemporary economics on this front, although their remedies are different. Other economists have lamented the decline in concern for policy relevance in economic theory. The long standing controversy about the realism of the assumptions that economists use in their theories resurfaces from time to time. A recent reincarnation of this issue by Dick Levins has emphasized the problem of drawing policy inferences from models with premises that are admittedly arbitrary, with parameters estimated with data of questionable quality and relevance.

John Maynard Keynes was an early critic of the application of statistical methods to economics. His review (Keynes, 1939) of Professor Tinbergen's book *A Method and its Application to Investment Activity* anticipates the issues raised in more contemporary writings. Keynes makes an important, but often neglected distinction between the logic of theory appraisal and the algebra of theory appraisal. In the context of econometric estimation, the logic of theory appraisal is concerned with the basis of inferences about cause and effect relationships that are drawn from correlations among variables. The algebra of theory appraisal, in contrast, is concerned with how these correlations are calculated. Keynes argues that statistical methods can, at best, give an indication of the strength of causal relationships among variables, and this can only be accomplished under what would seem to be unusual conditions. Statistical evidence cannot confirm nor can it disprove the structure of causal relationships derived from a theory. The 'method of multiple correlation' can be applied only after the economist has 'correctly analyzed beforehand the qualitative character of the causal relations' (p. 560) and after a complete enumeration of those factors that influence the variables in question. Unless the list is complete, and as well, unless the factors in the list are quantifiable, results of correlation calculations fall victim to what is now called missing variable bias. Keynes's assessment of the application of statistical methods advocated by Tinbergen is

> The method is one neither of discovery nor of criticism. It is a means of giving quantitative precision to what, in qualitative terms, we know already as the result of a complete theoretical analysis – provided always that it is the case where the other considerations to be given below are satisfied. (Keynes, 1939, p. 560)

The other considerations include the requirement that the causal factors are in fact independent of one another, that the historical period from which data are taken and the period for which predictions are being made are, 'in all relevant respects', homogeneous, and the variation in both those factors designated as causal and those interpreted as caused is informative enough to permit estimation of the relationships among them. Keynes points out that several of the results reported by Tinbergen seem to be fragile. Parameter values are not robust with respect to the time period used for estimation nor to the assumed structure of lag lengths. 'Professor Tinbergen's Method' was written over a half century ago. The capacity of economists to extract inferences from reluctant data has grown dramatically in the meantime. But many of the concerns that Keynes raised in 1939 are as relevant today as they were then.

ECONOMETRIC CONFESSIONS

Edward Leamer's essay 'Let's Take the Con Out of Econometrics' (Leamer, 1983) has become a modern classic. Professor Leamer's description of the state of empirical economics is far from flattering.

> This is a sad and decidedly unscientific state of affairs we find ourselves in. Hardly anyone takes data analyses seriously. Or perhaps more accurately, hardly anyone takes anyone else's data analyses seriously. Like elaborately plumed birds who have long since lost the ability to procreate but not the desire, we preen and strut and display our t-values. (p. 37)

If we cannot convince each other that the results of our econometric work are well-grounded, how can we convince non-technical audiences? Part of the econometrician's credibility problem stems from the problems of confounding and collinearity that typically plague the use of historical, as opposed to experimental, data. But Leamer is more concerned about the lack of transparency or perhaps the extent of empirical self-delusion practised by econometricians. According to his assessment, economists have sacrificed too much in fealty to the 'false idol of objectivity'. He enjoins his fellow practitioners to acknowledge that

> All knowledge is human belief; more accurately, human opinion. What often happens in the natural sciences is that there is a high degree of conformity of opinion. When this occurs, the opinion held by most is asserted to be an objective fact, and those who doubt it are labelled 'nuts'. But history is replete with examples of opinions losing majority status, with once objective 'truths' shrinking into the dark corners of social discourse. (p. 36)

Estimation of econometric models involves specification searches that are widely acknowledged to violate the axioms of statistical theory. This statistical theory is subsequently used to conduct hypothesis tests on the 'best' version of the model. Specification searches often reveal that what appear to be minor variations in model structure or in the definition of variables can overturn crucial empirical results. Econometric inference appears fragile.

Leamer argues that economists cannot escape from the influence of intuition, conjecture or opinion, and that they are foolhardy to try. A preferred approach would be to make the relationship between opinion and inference more explicit. In his words,

> What I propose to do is to develop a correspondence between regions in the assumption space and regions in the inference space. I will report that all assumptions in a certain set lead to essentially the same inference. Or I will report that there are assumptions within the set under consideration that lead to radically different inferences. (p. 38)

This is the job of the empirical researcher. Until this task is more broadly embraced, econometric inference is not likely to escape from its reputation for 'whimsy and fragility'.

William Dewald, Jerry Thursby and Richard Anderson's (1986) investigation of replication in empirical economic research raises troubling questions about the scientific practice of empirical economists. Their study was motivated by the presumption that empirical replication of the results obtained by other investigators is one of the hallmarks of any field that wishes to be considered scientific. Dewald *et al.* used data collected from papers published in the *Journal of Money, Credit and Banking*. The *Journal*'s editorial policy requires authors to submit computer programs and data sets used to obtain empirical results reported in manuscripts. They concluded that errors in programming and in data interpretation may be commonplace in published empirical work. In the nine studies that they examined in detail, exact replication was obtained in only two instances. 'Almost exact' replication was achieved in two more cases. In the remaining five studies, replication was not possible. In one case, attempts at replication reversed the published findings of the original paper. Reasons varied for this failure. Computer errors in the original work were identified. Reconstruction of the original data series was not possible in at least one case. Incompatibility of computer software made replication problematical in at least one instance. Apart from the nine studies for which replication was attempted, Dewald *et al.* requested original programs and data sets for all empirical studies published in the *Journal* after 1980. A disquieting number of authors never replied to repeated requests. Several authors who did respond indicated that their data had been lost or discarded since their paper was published. This would seem to raise the question of whether economists even take their own data analyses seriously.

Fischer Black (1982) draws a link between the non-experimental sources of data employed by economists and the problems of characterizing cause and effect relationships among variables from such data. Although the language of econometric estimation often obscures this fact, in Black's judgement, almost every econometric model is an attempt to interpret correlation as signifying causation. For example, 'exogenous' variables really mean 'causing' variables. 'Endogenous' variables are 'caused' variables.

The identification problem is really a general statement of the problem of drawing causal inferences from correlations among non-experimental data. Most econometric work involves the estimation of two, or more, relationships that involve an overlapping set of variables, such as demand and supply functions. Both depend on the price of the relevant commodity. Observations on price and quantity alone are not rich enough to disentangle movements in either variable into demand-induced and supply-induced changes. The standard remedy for the identification problem is to rig the structure of the relationships that involve the overlapping variables so that each relationship depends on enough other factors that exhibit enough of the right kind of variation. If this practice appears arbitrary to non-practitioners, perhaps this is because it is. But, according to the well-worn maxim, 'correlation does not imply causation'. The nature of economic theory may in fact compound the problems of interpretation of correlation. Black discusses several examples, including the relationships between advertising and sales, money supply and aggregate economic activity, consumption and output, inflation and exchange rates, taxes and work and generally, supply and demand, in which economic theory is equivocal in its interpretation of what is cause and what is effect. Do firms advertise products that they anticipate will generate higher sales, or does advertising cause higher sales? Or do cause and effect run both ways?

Interpretation of correlation in terms of cause and effect is made more difficult by most of the familiar problems of econometric estimation. Observed correlations between two variables may be the result of the influence of a third variable that has not been measured or that does not appear in the model. Errors in the observation of variables may produce phantom correlations, or may make actual correlations more difficult to detect. Correlations are often observed to be quite unstable over time. Black is not sanguine about the state of empirical work in economics. He concludes his essay with an admission that he has not been able to identify any generally satisfactory solution to these problems.

The title of David Hendry's essay 'Econometrics – Alchemy or Science?', is discomforting to the aspirations of economists who see their subject as scientific. Even though he quickly proceeds to explain that the current reputation of alchemy is not deserved, many respected scientists of old were interested in the field, it is too late. The damage to our collective self-esteem has been done. Unlike Keynes, Hendry subscribes to the view that empirical analysis can, at least in principle, be used to test the validity of economic theory. The body of his paper, however, emphasizes the limited progress that has been made in this endeavour since the exchange between Keynes and Tinbergen. Hendry enumerates empirical results that are not robust with respect to small changes in data or in model structure, the poor performance of econometric models when they are used for policy analysis[1] or the production of results that are conditioned on political beliefs or on preconceptions of the structure of the economy. Hendry concludes that it is too early to embrace either a negative or an affirmative answer to the question that he poses in his title. He is optimistic, but acknowledges that much current practice is not as helpful as it could be and that much remains to be done.

A Question of Emphasis

Wassily Leontief's criticism of the relationship between economic theory and economic observation has more to do with relative emphasis. Leontief was an early critic of what he saw as an unproductive trend in economic research. His American Economic Association presidential address of 1970 outlined several concerns. Leontief revisited these themes in a letter to the editor of *Science* in 1982. Leontief's Presidential Address is widely quoted by agricultural economists, a group held up by Leontief as a good example of how economic research should be conducted, but the influence of this essay on the economics profession in general has been negligible. Leontief took aim at the '*inadequacy* of the scientific means' (1971, p. 1) that limit the ability of economists to address contemporary economic problems. His conclusion is that 'The weak and all too slowly growing empirical foundation clearly cannot support the proliferating superstructure of pure, or should I say, speculative economic theory' (1971, p. 1). Leontief reopens the controversy associated with Friedman's (1953) influential essay regarding the empirical verification of assumptions. Rejecting Friedman's conclusion, Leontief asserts that 'it is precisely the empirical validity of these *assumptions* on which the usefulness of the entire exercise (i.e. academic economic model building) depends' (1971, p. 2). Novelty, not usefulness or successful verification drives the succession of models in the literature. According to Leontief, the academic reward system is in part responsible, but he also mentions a lack of commitment by federal and state governments to systematic and consistent data collection.

Leontief sustains his sharply critical tone in his 1982 *Science* letter. He begins by quoting with apparent approval the *Business Week* (18 January 1982, p. 124) assessment of the annual meetings of the American Economic Association. This gathering of academic economists is summarily dismissed as of little interest to outsiders. Leontief's diagnosis is that this moribund condition is a consequence of a widespread reluctance on the part of economists to participate in 'systematic empirical inquiry'. He supports this claim with a statistical description of the types of articles published in the *American Economic Review* in the 1970s and 1980s. More than half of the articles published in the *Review* during this period reported mathematical models without any data. Leontief describes a sort of empirical doldrums gripping the profession in which half-hearted efforts to glean insights from repeated dredging of essentially the same data sets is the high water mark of the empirical work.

The track record of hypothesis tests of central elements of neoclassical theory is not an enviable one.[2] Appelbaum (1978) and Fox and Kivanda (1994) urge caution in the application of the theory of the firm. Cozzarin and Gilmour (forthcoming) render a similar verdict for the theory of consumption and demand. If most economists consider the scientific credentials of their subject to be based in some way on the testing of theories and models against facts, these diagnoses should be troubling. The relationship between theory and observation continues to be problematical. Misgivings about the nature of this relationship undermine the authority of economists when they speak of matters of private and public policy.

The reasons for the track record of empirical economics are familiar to economists. Economic data are largely non-experimental. Experiments are conducted to isolate and measure the strength of hypothesized causal relationships. Economic data, being largely historical, are therefore often confounded, uninformative and incomplete. Historical data may be intercorrelated, making it difficult to separate the individual contributions of factors. Historical data may exhibit variation that renders them less than ideal for estimation. One variable may have an important causal effect on another variable, but may have exhibited little variation during the sample period. This makes it difficult to estimate, or even to identify the magnitude of the cause and effect relationship. Economic data are often collected for purposes other than economic research. Economists are frequently required to get by with surrogates and proxies for the variables that they really want to use in their models. And data collected for other purposes may not have been collected with the utmost attention to consistency and accuracy.

THE FRAGMENTATION OF MACROECONOMICS

Another factor that has shaken the collective confidence of economists is the disintegration of macroeconomics as an integrated body of knowledge. The macroeconomic debates between the monetarists and the Keynesians that dominated the literature and the textbooks of the 1960s and 1970s appear minor relative to the state of discourse in macroeconomics more recently. When I was in graduate school at the University of Minnesota in the early 1980s, I was fortunate enough to take a course in macroeconomic theory from Tom Sargent. He had just returned from an extended visit to several economics departments in the eastern United States. One day, one of my classmates asked him to comment on what he had learned during his trip. He replied that he was disappointed that no one at the schools that he had visited seemed to be doing macroeconomic theory any more. I presume that this was intended as jest, but like most humour, it also contained an element of sincerity.[3] In 1981, Daniel Bell and Irving Kristol edited a volume of essays under the title *The Crisis in Economic Theory*. The motivation for the volume was the erosion of confidence in the Keynesian synthesis of macroeconomic theory and policy that was forged by Hicks, Hansen and expounded by Samuelson in his influential *Principles* text. By 1981, it was apparent, at least to Bell and Kristol, that there was a need to examine the fundamental assumptions and the structure of the model that had been so influential in guiding national macroeconomic policies in the post-war era. The issues that Bell and Kristol raise, however, were not new to the 1980s. The nature and empirical relevance of the concept of equilibrium, the tension between aggregate and individualistic approaches to economic modelling and explanation, the relationship between macroeconomic and microeconomic theory, the degree to which actual human behaviour corresponds to economists' characterization of rationality as optimization and the way that economic theory should address the role of time, imperfect information and expectations are all identified in the opening chapter of the book as pressing theoretical questions. Bell and Kristol fail to acknowledge that these questions have a long history in economic controversies.

PROBLEMS WITH THE PEDAGOGY OF ECONOMICS

> To say something is wrong with graduate education is to say that something is wrong with the economics profession. (Robert Solow, quoted in Klamer and Colander, 1990, p. 18)

In the December 1993 issue of the *American Economic Review*, 463 economics professors, who identified themselves as undergraduate teachers, presented a petition calling for the reform of graduate education in economics. Many of the concerns that they identify echo the issues raised by Klamer and Colander.[4] As faculty involved in recruiting and hiring recent PhDs, the petition signatories would prefer to consider candidates for faculty positions that possessed:

1. familiarity with the major economic debates that have occurred within the past 20 years and an understanding of the ways in which those debates have shaped the beliefs of economists,
2. a grounding in the models that are actually used to teach undergraduates,
3. knowledge of important economic institutions and the role that those institutions play in the economy,
4. skills of oral and written communication, especially as these skills relate to the content of the undergraduate curriculum,
5. knowledge of alternative approaches to economics and an ability to compare and contrast those approaches,
6. knowledge of econometrics, including an appreciation of the limits of econometric testing.

This petition was motivated by a belief that many PhD candidates currently lack some or all of these capabilities and as a consequence are not well suited to the task of undergraduate instruction, a task that absorbs a significant share of the time of many junior faculty.

The 1993 petition was preceded by Colander's and Klamer's (1987) survey of attitudes and impressions of students in six top-ranked graduate programs in economics in the United States.[5] Their findings give a revealing perspective on the process of education and socialization of prospective PhDs. Many students expressed a sense of tension between the need to learn techniques and methods and a desire to do policy-relevant research. Students perceived a lack of emphasis on understanding the historical context of the theories that they were studying. Knowledge of institutions or an understanding of how an actual economy works was not seen as important. Comments from interviews and small group discussions indicate that the graduate students of the mid–1980s were assimilating the academic pecking order that Leijonhufvud (1975) caricatured a decade earlier. Colander and Klamer witnessed a high level of scepticism among the graduate students that they interviewed. They got the impression that these students were coming to see research as a type of game, played out for its own sake.[6]

Colander and Klamer observed a great deal of variation on substantive issues among students at different schools. For example, 70 per cent of the students at Chicago agreed that minimum wages increased unemployment among young and unskilled workers, compared to 15 per cent at Harvard. None of the students at MIT thought that the rational expectations assumption was important, but 59 per cent of the students at Chicago did. Chicago students' responses were consistently different from those of their colleagues at other schools on several topics. They also reported a much lower level of tension between what they were learning in their courses and their research and career interests.

A symposium sponsored by the National Science Foundation in 1986 served as a forum to discuss the state of graduate education in economics. A sufficient number of participants expressed the view that graduate training had become too detached from real world problems to prompt Robert Eisner, the president of the American Economic Association, to appoint a Commission on Graduate Education in Economics in 1988. The report of the Commission was published in the *Journal of Economic Literature* in 1991 (Krueger *et al.*; Hansen, Kasper *et al.*). The findings of the Commission confirmed much of what the Colander and Klamer study had found. Graduates from graduate programmes in economics are facing more and more competition in the job market from students from business schools and programmes in public administration. Graduate course work in economics emphasizes tools and theory, along with proficiency in mathematics, at the expense of creativity, communication ability and problem solving skills. New PhDs typically have only limited understanding of important economic institutions. What is most disturbing in the Commission's findings, however, is the perception shared by faculty and students alike, that the current regime of course work and comprehensive exams is not doing very much at all to prepare students to actually do original research.

The results of the Colander and Klamer study and the findings of the Commission on Graduate Education in Economics are certainly no basis for complacency. Employers, students and an increasing number of faculty are expressing dissatisfaction with the status quo. Many of the recommendations arising out of this literature relate to the way in which graduate education is managed. Students should be expected to write more at the earlier stages of their graduate programmes. Curriculum in core courses should be seen as a departmental responsibility, not the prerogative of individual instructors. But some of these issues are more fundamental. Is an understanding of the operation of a market economy or is knowledge of the characteristics of actual social institutions useful in the development or in the validation of economic theory? What is the relationship between theory and observation? What is the appropriate degree of formalism in economic theory? There are important methodological roots to this growing dissatisfaction.

POLICY RELEVANCE VERSUS FORMALISM

Terence Hutchison's (1992) *Changing Aims in Economics* is also critical of trends in university training in economics. He argues that a fundamental shift occurred in the purpose of academic economic research and teaching after World War II. Hutchison contends that from the time of Sir William Petty, whom he identifies as the first economist, the primary aim of economic inquiry was to improve government policy decisions. He contends that economists have been moving away from this aim over the last half century. He calls this the 'Formalist Revolution'. The hallmarks of this revolution are the pursuit of abstract formal analysis of models with no prospect of practical benefit and a general impatience with painstaking empirical and institutional work. Hutchison documents a growing chorus of dissent to this trend which he dates from about 1970. Benjamin Ward's *What's Wrong With Economics?*, Leontief's American Economic Association presidential address, Ragnar Frisch's critique of 'playometrics', as well as essays by Worswick (1972), Clower (1989), Sir Henry Phelps Brown (1972) and Klamer and Colander (1990) are cited in support of Hutchison's unhappy diagnosis. Abandonment of the aim of policy relevance and the emphasis of technique over substance has contributed to what Kuttner (1985) describes as 'departments of economics are graduating a generation of *idiots savants* brilliant at esoteric mathematics yet innocent of actual economic life'; Hutchison traces this pathology to errors in methodology. Richard Levins has touched on these themes, and in the process sparked a lively exchange among agricultural economists, with two controversial essays, 'On Farmers Who Solve Equations' (1989)[7] and 'The Whimsical Science' (1992). In 'On Farmers', Levins takes aim at Milton Friedman's famous and influential position regarding the realism of assumptions.[8] According to the popular interpretation of Friedman, it makes perfect sense for economists to assume that rational human behaviour can be represented 'as if' people solve mathematical optimization problems. Levins argues that in invoking this metaphorical 'as if' argument, much of the use of mathematics in economic models gives a false impression of rigour. The critical logical step in relating the results of an abstract mathematical model to a particular instance of human behaviour is the demonstration that some or all of the properties of the mathematical model correspond to elements of the actual situation being studied. Invoking the 'as if' metaphor, in Levins's assessment, is not an adequate demonstration of correspondence.

Levins's papers and the exchange that they precipitated are not without precedent. David Novick published a two page note in the *Review of Economics and Statistics* in November 1954. Novick had the temerity to suggest that mathematics is a type of shorthand in the social sciences. It serves as an alternative way of expressing what has become known through other means. He also contends that some of the practitioners of a mathematical approach to economics have stumbled over some basics of logic. In particular, he criticizes the practice of proceeding 'from theory to proof to application without recognizing the intervening steps that usually must be worked out'. He accuses economists of following the example of their colleagues in the natural sciences, but only in part. He suggests that this propensity has sometimes given an unwarranted look of definitiveness of knowledge about actual economic phenomena. This brief and, to my reading modest, note was met with no fewer than nine comments by prominent economists.[9] The comments were coordinated by Paul Samuelson himself.

Alexander Rosenberg contends that economics is not an empirical science and that it cannot become one, given the current methodological views of its practitioners. He considers economics to be a branch of mathematics with tenuous links to empirical phenomena.

Much of the mystery surrounding the actual development of economic theory – its shifts in formalism, its insulation from empirical assessment, its interest in proving purely formal abstract possibilities, its unchanged character over a period of centuries, the controversies about its cognitive status – can be comprehended and properly appreciated if we give up the notion that economics any longer has the aims or makes the claims of an empirical science of human behaviour. Rather we should view it as a branch of mathematics, one devoted to examining the formal properties of a set of abstract relations: axioms that implicitly define a technical notion of 'rationality', just as geometry examines the formal properties of abstract points and lines. This abstract term 'rationality' may have far more potential interpretations than economists realize, but rather less bearing on human behaviour and its consequences than we have unreasonably demanded economists reveal. (1983, p. 311)

Rosenberg acknowledges that this interpretation of the scientific credentials of economics leaves a public policy vacuum.

IS THERE A CRISIS IN ECONOMICS?

A list of titles that includes *The Crisis in Economic Theory* (Bell and Kristol eds, 1981), *What's Wrong With Economics?* (Ward, 1972), *Economics on Trial: Lies, Myths and Realities* (Skousen, 1991) and 'The Whimsical Science' (Levins, 1992), suggests that all is not well in the community of worldly philosophers. A growing number of prominent economists is expressing concern about trends in economic research and teaching. It is the thesis of this book that this dissent is animated, at least in part, by methodological questions. What is the purpose of economic inquiry? What is the appropriate role of abstraction in economic theory? What are the admissible sources of economic knowledge? Is economics a science? Can it be? Should it be? The encouraging sign in the midst of a growing body of critical literature regarding the state of economics is an increasingly active scholarship in economic methodology. After several decades of neglect or persecution, it is becoming more accepted for economists with more philosophical predilections to raise questions about methodology. In the immediate postwar era, the first chapter of Paul Samuelson's *Foundations of Economic Analysis* (1947/1965) and Friedman's 1953 essay seemed to be all the necessary methodological equipment that economists required. But the lid on that toolbox was rarely opened, as a high level of professional consensus on matters methodological had been achieved. From Schumpeter, we accepted the argument that the science of economics would advance using the mathematical, statistical and empirical methods that had served the natural sciences so well. Theory development and validation was to proceed, following Samuelson and Hutchison, by deriving and testing falsifiable hypotheses. From Friedman, economists took as self-evident truth that the assumptions or axioms used in a theory were 'as - if' statements that were not only not intended to be true descriptions of reality, but in fact were more valuable as the degree of descriptive accuracy decreased. And finally, from Robbins we understood our subject matter to be human behaviour in the allocation of scarce means among competing ends.

Beginning in the 1970s, however, this majority view began to erode. Critics of the mainstream from without were not uncommon up to this point, but the incidence of friendly fire began to increase. Table 1.1 lists selected contributions to the growing methodological literature since 1970. If economic theory is not in the midst of a philosophical crisis, what is the motivation behind the writers that have contributed to this literature?

The purpose of this book is neither to bury the reputation of economics nor to praise it. My goal is to examine economists' claims regarding the scientific credentials of their subject. This is a book about methodology. It is about the ways that economists try to evaluate theories and the relationship between those theories and the phenomena that they are intended to represent. In the next chapter, I explore an important aspect of the reputation of economists. It is the stuff of legend that economists are a factious bunch, seldom able to agree on anything. Recent surveys of economists' opinions challenge this perception. Economists seem to agree on many things. But the basis for this agreement is often obscure. Economists claim to know certain things about the way the world works. But how do they know what they know? Chapter 3 is an introduction to the study of methodology or the philosophy of science as related to economics. There seem to be four watershed methodological questions that divide economists:

- What is the purpose of economic inquiry?
- What are the legitimate sources of economic knowledge?
- What is the scope of application of economic knowledge?

and

- What is the appropriate structure of an economic theory?

Chapters 4 to 8 survey the major schools of thought on the philosophy of economics, largely organized around how proponents of each of these schools answer these four questions. The final chapter of the book attempts to synthesize what we know about the scientific status of economics as a discipline.

Clichés about the lack of value of the study of the methodology of economics are commonplace. They are popular fare among economists giving addresses in plenary sessions at professional meetings. But witty remarks will not make challenges to the scientific status of our discipline go away. They will not bridge the gulf between economic theory and economic data. They will not resolve the enduring and fundamental disagreements that undermine the influence of economists' pronouncements on policy issues.

QUESTIONS FOR DISCUSSION

1. List the most important empirical papers in your area of specialization. What impact have these papers had on policy? At what level?
2. Is it important that economics be considered a science? Why?
3. How does your experience as a student of economics compare with the results of the Colander and Klamer survey? Would you have signed the 1993 AEA petition?
4. Is economics in a crisis?

NOTES

1. Hendry mentions Goodhart's (1978) treatment of this problem but not Lucas's (1980).
2. This topic will be revisited in Chapter 4.
3. One of my graduate students once told me that during his academic career he had taken ten courses in macroeconomics and the only thing they had in common was the name.
4. David Colander signed the 1993 *American Economic Review* petition.
5. Students from the University of Chicago, Columbia University, Harvard University, the Massachusetts Institute of Technology, Stanford University and Yale University were included in the sample. Klamer and Colander reported the findings of their survey in more detail in a book they published in 1990, and David Colander and Reuven Brenner (1992) edited a volume of papers from a conference on the state of graduate education in economics.
6. Colander and Klamer mentioned that students at the University of Chicago and at George Mason University differed from students at the other schools that they visited. Students at these two schools were described at 'true believers'.
7. This essay precipitated a series of comments and replies that were published in several subsequent issues of the magazine *Choices*.
8. Friedman's views on the methodology of economics are investigated at length in Chapter 5.
9. Including, by my reckoning, at least five eventual Nobel Prize recipients!

2. How do Economists Know What They Know?

Disagreement among economists is legendary. The limited amount of economist humour is largely based on this professional reputation. Some examples include: 'If you were to lay all of the economists in the world end to end, you would never reach a conclusion', and 'If you put five economists in a room, you will have seven opinions, and two of those will belong to John Maynard Keynes', and there is the story about a former US president that said that he had searched his entire professional life for a one-armed economist. This chapter examines this unfortunate reputation of economists, not so much to confirm or to contradict its validity or its fairness, but to examine the basis for the agreement that has been observed. It turns out that economists agree on many things. There is a perplexing level of international variation in the degree of agreement. But the actual degree of consensus belies the economists' reputation for factiousness.

What is less clear is why economists agree when they do agree. Do they agree because they accept the results of successful predictions derived from economic theories? Is consensus reached because of the results of controlled experiments reported in the leading journals of the profession? Do they agree on the basis of hypothesis tests conducted with historical data and econometric techniques? Or does the observed degree of consensus arise through the consistent use of deductive logic starting from a set of true axioms about human behaviour?

HOW DO WE KNOW WHAT ECONOMISTS KNOW?

If we were in possession of an encyclopaedic statement of true knowledge of economic phenomena, then we could assess what economists know by comparing what they say to this true knowledge. Unfortunately, such an encyclopaedia is not available. Alternatively, we could observe the number of times economists respond 'I don't know' when asked to comment on some issue. As it turns out, however, 'I don't know' is a rare response. This is true even when a large fraction of economists know that a statement is wrong and an equally large group knows that it is correct. So I have elected to use

consensus as indicative of knowledge. If a significant degree of consensus is obtained on a particular statement, I shall conclude that economists know that a statement is either true or false, depending on the polarization of the agreement.

Understanding the *basis* for agreement among economists is difficult, however. Ronald Coase (1982) describes three important episodes in the recent history of economic thought. In the discussion to follow, I argue that Coase's stories contradict the popular understanding of how scientific progress occurs. They also are inconsistent with the modern methodological orthodoxy that economists claim to support.

THE AMERICAN ECONOMIC ASSOCIATION SURVEY – 1976

Kearl *et al.* (1979) were the first to examine the reputation of their profession empirically. They were concerned with two perceptions about economists. First, that economists are hopelessly divided on many major policy issues and second, that economists devote most of their research efforts to solving arcane technical puzzles that appear to have little relevance to current social problems. In the Kearl *et al.* study, members of the American Economic Association were asked what they thought on a variety of subjects. A stratified random sample of 600 US-based members of the American Economic Association were asked to 'Generally agree', 'Agree with provisions' or 'Generally disagree' with 30 statements. These statements spanned a wide range of economic issues from the effects of trade restrictions on general economic welfare to the legitimacy of government efforts to redistribute income. Armed in part with Friedman's explanation of why economists disagree,[1] Kearl *et al.* hypothesized that survey respondents would exhibit greater consensus on positive statements, that is, statements about what is, than on normative statements, that is, statements about what ought to be. They also anticipated that economists would agree more on statements related to microeconomics than to macroeconomics.

The Kearl *et al.* study found that US economists exhibited a statistically significant degree of consensus on 20 of the 30 propositions on the questionnaire. The 20 consensus propositions are listed in Table 2.1. Given the degree of popular controversy surrounding some of these issues, the uniformity of economists' responses to some of these 20 statements is remarkable. The fact that only 3 per cent of respondents generally disagreed with the statement that 'Tariffs and import quotas reduce economic welfare' and that 2 per cent generally disagreed that 'A ceiling on rents reduces the quantity and quality of housing available' sets economists apart from the

Table 2.1   Statements on which consensus exists* among US-based American Economics Association members – 1976 survey

Statement	Consensus Position	Extent of Dissent	Category
Tariffs and import quotas reduce economic welfare	Agree	3% Generally disagree	Micro, positive
The government should be an employer of last resort and initiate a guaranteed job programme	Disagree	26% Generally agree	Macro, normative
The money supply is a more important target than interest rates for monetary policy	Agree	29% Generally disagree	Macro, positive
Cash payments are superior to transfers in kind	Agree	8% Generally disagree	Micro, positive
Flexible exchange rates offer an effective international monetary arrangement	Agree	5% Generally disagree	Micro, positive
The 'Corporate State' as depicted by Galbraith accurately describes the context and structure of the US economy	Disagree	18% Generally agree	Micro, positive
A minimum wage increases unemployment among young and unskilled workers	Agree	10% Generally disagree	Micro, positive
Fiscal policy has a significant stimulative impact on a less than fully employed economy	Agree	8% Generally disagree	Macro, positive
Antitrust laws should be used vigorously to reduce monopoly power from its current level	Agree	15% Generally disagree	Micro, normative
The government should restructure the welfare system along lines of a 'negative income tax'	Agree	8% Generally disagree	Macro, normative
Wage-price controls should be used to control inflation	Disagree	6% Generally	—

Statement	Consensus Position	Extent of Dissent	Category
A ceiling on rents reduces the quantity and quality of housing available	Agree	2% Generally disagree	Micro, positive
The Fed should be instructed to increase the money supply at a fixed rate	Disagree	14% Generally agree	Macro, normative
Effluent taxes represent a better approach to pollution control than imposition of pollution ceilings	Agree	19% Generally disagree	Micro, positive
Reducing the regulatory power of the ICC, CAB *et al.* would improve the efficiency of the US economy	Agree	22% Generally disagree	Micro, normative
The federal budget should be balanced over the business cycle rather than yearly	Agree	17% Generally disagree	Macro, normative
The fundamental cause of the rise in oil prices of the past three years is the monopoly power of the large oil companies	Disagree	11% Generally agree	—
The redistribution of income is a legitimate role for government in the context of the US economy	Agree	19% Generally disagree	—
The ceiling on interest paid on time deposits should be removed	Agree	6% Generally disagree	Micro, normative
'Consumer protection' laws generally reduce economic efficiency	Disagree	24% Generally agree	—

Notes
* As reported by Kearl *et al.* (1979) based on a Kolmorgorov-Smirnov test at a 1 per cent significance level.

Source: Based on Kearl *et al.* (1979).

general population on these two issues. Kearl *et al.* argued that their results indicate a high degree of consensus on several fundamental issues and emphasized the broad professional support for the price system as an instrument of social coordination. Responses to the statements about trade restrictions, minimum wages, antitrust laws, rent controls, wage and price controls, effluent taxes, regulatory reform, oil prices and monopolies and interest rate ceilings were seen as supporting the effective operation of the market process.

Kearl *et al.* concluded that Friedman's hypothesis that economists agree on positive propositions to a greater degree than they do on normative statements was confirmed by their data. They also concluded that responses to macroeconomic propositions were more divergent than on microeconomic issues. Overall, the authors of the Kearl study contended that the reputation of economists for divisiveness is unjustified. However, they also acknowledged that economists have not achieved consensus on several important current public policy issues. For example, survey responses did not exhibit agreement on the statement that the distribution of income should be more equal in the United States, on the proposition that US defence expenditures should be reduced, on the Phillips curve short-run trade-off between inflation and unemployment, or on the need to curtail the economic power of unions. Journalists and politicians seeking wisdom on these important and practical matters would suffer from an abundance of professional opinions, but no consistent answers if they were to approach members of the American Economic Association.

INTERNATIONAL SURVEY

Five years after the publication of the Kearl *et al.* study, Frey *et al.* (1984) reported the results of a similar international poll. A questionnaire, modelled on Kearl *et al.*, was sent to a stratified random sample of the members of the relevant associations of professional economists in the United States, France, West Germany, Austria and Switzerland. Three propositions from the earlier study which related to particular events and institutions in the United States were deleted. Minor variations in wording were made in the remaining 27 statements. Based on analysis of the entire sample of 936 responses, the Frey group found some similarities to the patterns of consensus reported in the Kearl *et al.* study. The seven statements with the highest degree of agreement internationally (as measured by relative entropy) are reported in descending order of consensus in Table 2.2. The proposition with the lowest level of consensus, again measured by relative entropy, was 'The government should restructure the welfare system along the lines of a "negative income tax"'. Three statements with equally divergent responses followed, 'Cash payments

Table 2.2 Statements with the highest degree of consensus in an international survey of economists

Proposition	Consensus position	Extent of dissent
Wage-price controls should be used to control inflation	Disagree	9.8% Generally agree
The fundamental cause of the rise in oil prices of the past five years is the monopoly power of the large oil companies	Disagree	9.3% Generally agree
'Consumer protection' laws generally reduce economic efficiency	Disagree	13.6% Generally agree
Tariffs and import quotas reduce general economic welfare	Agree	10.3% Generally disagree
A ceiling on rents reduces the quantity and quality of housing available	Agree	15.0% Generally disagree
Antitrust laws should be used vigorously to reduce monopoly power from its current level	Agree	12.5% Generally disagree
The federal budget should be balanced over the business cycle rather than yearly	Agree	15.5% Generally disagree

Source: Based on Frey *et al.* (1984), Table 1, ranking based on reported relative entropy scores.

are superior to transfers-in kind', 'Effluent taxes represent a better approach to pollution control than imposition of pollution ceilings', and 'Reducing the influence of regulatory authorities ... would improve the efficiency of the economy'. These were followed by 'The distribution of income in the developed industrial nations should be more equal' and 'In the short run, unemployment can be reduced by increasing the rate of inflation', which were ranked equally on the relative entropy criterion.

Unlike the Kearl *et al.* study, Frey *et al.* found no statistically significant difference between the levels of consensus on positive and normative propositions or on macroeconomic and microeconomic statements. What is perhaps even more interesting are the differences in patterns of consensus among the nations represented in the sample. Table 2.3 contrasts responses to six questions on which US economists exhibited a high degree of consensus. Results of a survey of Canadian economists conducted by Block and Walker (1988) are also included in the table. Canadian and German economists responded with a high degree of consensus on the issue of tariffs and import quotas, but this accord erodes for European economists outside Germany. French economists in particular showed no consistent position on this issue and more than 26 per cent of respondents from France generally disagreed with the statement. On the effect of rent controls on the supply of housing, the US, German and Canadian economists were almost unanimous, while the French and to a lesser extent the Swiss and Austrians dissembled.

Whether the degree of uniformity of responses of an international sample of economists is impressive or worrisome is in the eye of the beholder. The international variation in professional opinion on some basic issues does raise important questions on the scientific status of economic knowledge. How can a scientific statement about some economic phenomenon be true in the United States and not in France? Is human behaviour fundamentally different in the two countries? Does this mean that economic theory needs to be site-specific?

Equally worrisome as the international divergence of views is the indication, based on recent work by Alston *et al.* (1992), that the agreement among US economists is beginning to unravel (Table 2.4). All of the statements which received the most uniform responses in the 1976 survey of US economists met with a higher degree of dissent when the survey was repeated in 1990. Only time will tell if this trend will continue.

AGRICULTURAL ECONOMISTS

Pope and Hallam's (1986) survey of agricultural economists reveals another chink in the armour of professional consensus: inconsistency. In this study, a stratified sample of members of the American Agricultural Economics Association was asked to agree or disagree with 72 statements about govern-

Table 2.3 An international comparison of economists' views

Statement		United States	Austria	France	Germany	Switzerland	Canada
				Responses			
Tariffs and import quotas reduce general economic welfare	Consensus position	Agree	Agree	—	Agree	Agree	Agree
	Dissent	2.8% Generally disagree	13.2% Generally disagree	26.4% Generally disagree	5.5% Generally disagree	10.1% Generally disagree	3.8% Generally disagree
Cash payments are superior to transfers-in-kind	Consensus position	Agree	Agree	Agree	Agree	—	Agree
	Dissent	7.6% Generally disagree	18.7% Generally disagree	19.1% Generally disagree	20.5% Generally disagree	21.6% Generally disagree	12.4% Generally disagree
Flexible exchange rates offer an effective international monetary arrangement	Consensus position	Agree	Agree	—	Agree	Agree	Agree
	Dissent	4.7% Generally disagree	16.5% Generally disagree	44.4% Generally disagree	5.1% Generally disagree	7.5% Generally disagree	5.9% Generally disagree
Fiscal policy has a significant stimulativ impact on a less than fully employed economy	Consensus position	Agree	Agree	Agree	Agree	Agree	Agree
	Dissent	7.6% Generally disagree	6.6% Generally disagree	4.9% Generally disagree	11.7% Generally disagree	12.2% Generally disagree	14.2% Generally disagree
Wage-price control should be used to control inflation	Consensus position	Disagree	Disagree	—	Disagree	Disagree	Disagree
	Dissent	5.7% Generally agree	17.6% Generally agree	25.3% Generally agree	2.2% Generally agree	8.5% Generally agree	4.5% Generally agree
A ceiling on rents reduces the quantity and quality of housing available	Consensus position	Agree	Agree	—	Agree	Agree	Agree
	Dissent	1.9% Generally disagree	11% Generally disagree	43.8% Generally disagree	5.9% Generally disagree	19.6% Generally disagree	4.7% Generally disagree

Sources: Based on Frey et al. (1984, United States, Austria, France, Germany and Switzerland) and Block and Walker (1988, Canada).

25

Table 2.4   Changes in consensus among US economists 1976-1990

	Degree of Dissent	
Statement	1976	1990
Tariffs and import quotas reduce general economic welfare	3% Generally disagree	6.5% Generally disagree
Cash payments are superior to transfers-in-kind	8% Generally disagree	15.1% Generally disagree
Flexible exchange rates offer an effective international monetary arrangement	5% Generally disagree	8.4% Generally disagree
Fiscal policy has a significant stimulative impact on a less than fully employed economy	8% Generally disagree	9.1% Generally disagree
Wage-price controls should be used to control inflation	6% Generally agree	8.4% Generally agree
A ceiling on rents reduces the quantity and quality of housing available	2% Generally disagree	6.5% Generally disagree

Sources: 1976 – Kearl *et al.* (1979), 1990 – Alston *et al.* (1992).

ment policy, research methods and economic theory considered to be within the sphere of agricultural economists' professional interests. Pope and Hallam do not report relative entropy scores in their paper. In any case, they allowed five responses to each statement – Strongly Agree, Agree, Disagree, Strongly Disagree and Don't Know – and so entropy measures would not be readily comparable to the published surveys of general economists. Nevertheless, they identify ten statements which received reasonably uniform responses (Table 2.5) and nine statements on which the profession was deeply divided (Table 2.6). Seven of the ten assertions listed in Table 2.5 could be categorized as positive propositions. Normative statements on which agreement was observed involved support for trade liberalization, a rejection of consumer welfare as the sole criterion for the assessment of farm policy and support for growth of farm firms. At least five of the statements which divide the profession, however, are also positive. The questions that Pope and Hallam posed to their colleagues were much more specific than those used in the surveys discussed earlier. This makes it more difficult to draw inferences about the degree of professional support for the price system as an instrument of social coordination. In some instances, for example support for trade liberalization and opposition to measures to interfere with the growth of farm size, agricultural economists share general economists' confidence in the price system. The devil is in the details, however. Support for a range of government actions intended to mediate suspected market failures, for example subsidies for yield insurance, market intelligence and research and technology, indicates that agricultural economists frequently see pathologies in the price system. Of course, given the opportunity, general economists might provide similar responses to more specific questions.

CAUSES AND CONSEQUENCES OF CONSENSUS

Economists have been able to agree on certain issues to a degree that might surprise outsiders. This agreement is not complete, but on a number of significant practical issues the professional perspective of economists differs from many other social and professional groups. True, there are troubling inconsistencies. Why do economists seem to hold similar views on the effects of minimum wages and differ on the need to reduce the power of labour unions? How can agricultural economists be so united in their support of trade liberalization and at the same time be so deeply divided on whether market incentives lead to efficient use of agricultural resources?

How is it that economists have reached agreement on those basic propositions for which consensus has been observed? In principle, there are several ways in which this accord might have been reached. Compilation of the results of careful historical case studies, comparing jurisdictions which restricted imports and exports with those which did not, could have provided the basis for agreement on the virtue of free trade. A track record of successful predictions, for example that introduction of minimum wage laws would be followed by an increase in unemployment among young and unskilled workers, for a convincing set of situations, could also serve as a basis for professional consensus. On the other hand, repeated failure to reject hypotheses derived from theoretical models might have convinced economists that Galbraith's description of the structure of the US economy was inaccurate. It is even possible that economists have been persuaded by demonstrations of error-free deduction of conclusions from validated premises about human behaviour and interaction.

Coase (1982), however, has described three pivotal events in the history of economic thought that suggest that these factors may be overrated in the emergence of professional consensus among economists. In February of 1931,

Table 2.5: Consensus among agricultural economists

Proposition	Consensus position
Disaster and crop insurance programmes which are funded (partially or completely) by the government, raise social welfare as compared to a *laissez-faire* policy	61.6% Generally agree
Price supports have led to more stability in agricultural income as compared to a *laissez-faire* policy	61.2% Generally agree
Government data collection and analysis leads to an increase in market efficiency	61.6% Generally agree
Models of agricultural economic response based upon risk-averse behaviour are useful in positive economic analysis	69.4% Generally agree
Social welfare is improved through the provision and enforcement of antitrust laws	67.8% Generally agree
Free trade policies should be pursued by the federal government	66.5% Generally agree
Economic research supported by the experiment station is socially productive (that is, social costs are less than social benefits) and should be publicly funded	60.0% Generally agree
Marketing orders have succeeded in stabilizing and/or raising prices such that producers are better off	67.3% Generally agree
All agricultural policies should be evaluated only in terms of their ultimate effects on aggregate consumer welfare	64.5% Generally disagree
Society should not discourage farm growth	66.5% Generally agree

Source: Based on Pope and Hallam (1986).

Table 2.6: Dissension among agricultural economists

Proposition	% Agreeing or strongly agreeing	% Disagreeing or strongly disagreeing
Marketing orders which facilitate price bargaining improve social welfare	44.9	43.2
Governmental policies should not attempt to redistribute income and wealth from other sectors of the economy to factors of production in agriculture	50.6	42.4
Barriers to entry and exit in agricultural industries are sufficiently low that the markets can be characterized by what some economists have called contestable (approaching a competitive allocation of resources)	47.4	43.7
Market incentives do not lead to efficient conservation (use) of agricultural resources	44.5	48.1
Changes in the prices of agricultural outputs lead input price changes	37.9	41.3
Farm management issues and skills should be central to agricultural economic analysis	50.2	45.2
Dynamic optimization tools are primarily useful in normative, rather than positive, economic analysis	35.5	32.7
Agricultural decision makers process information in a simple way such that adaptive or static expectations, rather than rational expectations, best describe behaviour	32.3	38.9
Current public policy regarding grain and cotton production is socially preferred to a *laissez-faire* policy	42.4	42.4

Source: Based on Pope and Hallam (1986).

Hayek gave a series of lectures entitled 'Prices and Production' at the London School of Economics. Coase was affiliated with the LSE at that time. He recalls that

> What was said seemed to us of great importance and made us see things of which we had previously been unaware. After hearing these lectures, we knew why there was a depression. Most students of economics and many members of the staff became Hayekians. Hayek's analysis seemed to give a well organized and fruitful way of thinking about the working of the economic system as a whole. As far as I can see, Hayekian analysis did not make predictions except in the sense that it explained why there was a depression. (Coase, 1982)

Coase describes the influence of Hayek's lectures as 'local' but an enumeration of the economists associated with the LSE at the time reveals that this was an influential locality! For present purposes, I wish to emphasize the absence of at least three of the classic factors in the achievement of scientific consensus from Coase's account. What proved to be an internationally influential audience of economists was persuaded to embrace much of what Hayek said based not on results of the tests of hypotheses, or on historical case studies or successful predictions but on the basis of the comprehensiveness and the plausibility of the explanation.

The second episode, remarkable in relation to the brevity of the Hayekian revolution, was the rapid acceptance of Keynes's General Theory as an alternative to Hayek's business cycle theory. According to Coase

> The swift adoption of the Keynesian system came about ... because its analysis in terms of the determinants of effective demand seemed to get to the essence of what was going on in the economic system and was easier to understand (at least in its broad outlines) than alternative theories. That the Keynesian system offered a cure for unemployment without any sacrifices, provided a clearly defined role for government and a policy easy to carry out (as it then appeared), added to its attractiveness. (Coase, 1982)

Once again, Coase considers the fact that Keynes's analysis 'seemed to make more sense to most economists' as decisive.

The third episode, drawn as well from the early 1930s, involved the theories of imperfect competition of Chamberlin and Robinson. Coase attributes part of the success of these contributions in influencing the collective thinking of the economics profession to the fact that they fell on fertile soil. Widespread dissatisfaction with the condition of then existing price theory created a ready market for ideas. As in the two previous episodes, widespread acceptance of Chamberlin's and Robinson's views occurred rapidly and without the benefit of hypothesis tests, case studies or successful predictions.

IMPLICATIONS

Not one of Coase's three episodes from the mid-twentieth century history of economic thought conforms to the popular perception of the scientific method. Each represented a revolution in the thinking of economists, but none follow the Kuhnian model of a paradigm shift during a scientific revolution.

It is certainly not a boost to the professional confidence of economists to observe that, even in those areas where a reasonable degree of consensus exists, government policies have been stubbornly contrary to this collective wisdom. The postwar trend towards liberalization of international trade and the associated integration of national economies represents the steady but hard-fought triumph of economic ideas. However, each stage in the demolition of protectionism seems to resurrect the same old demons. And progress on rent controls and minimum wages has been negligible.

The ability of economists to reach durable and justified agreement on the fundamentals of economic knowledge and their ability to influence the private and more particularly the public choices of their contemporaries, hinges on the resolution of some basic methodological questions. Economists, if they aspire to bear the appellation 'scientists', need a general protocol for the authentication of economic knowledge claims. The profession presently suffers from an overabundance of competing protocols. The rest of this book is devoted to the description and criticism of the various methodological positions that have been proposed for a scientific economics. These schools offer very different answers to some fundamental philosophical and methodological questions. Each school makes distinctive claims about the origin of economic knowledge, about the appropriate structure of economic theories and about the ultimate purpose of economic inquiry. Modern methodological orthodoxy is actually an eclectic composite of ideas from different schools. What does not seem to be widely appreciated among economists is that these ideas are often incompatible and convey quite different notions about the authentication of knowledge claims. If economics is to take its desired place in the ranks of scientific disciplines, it will be necessary to resolve these competing claims.

QUESTIONS FOR DISCUSSION

1. What do you think accounts for the differences in consensus among economists from different countries?
2. Do you agree or disagree with the consensus views of Canadian or US economists?
3. What do you think leads to shifts in professional allegiance to theories among economists, such as the three incidents described by Coase?

NOTE

1. Friedman's (1953) hypothesis was that economists agree more on positive than on normative issues.

3. What is Methodology?

Methodology is concerned with whether the claims of economics are reliable and true and how one can judge whether they are reliable and true; and it is concerned with whether the practices of economists lead to conclusions that one ought to rely on or to believe. (Daniel Hausman, 1992, p. 264)

This is a book about the methodology of economics. This subject occupies an infrequently travelled middle ground between economics and the philosophy of science. Few philosophers of science have investigated the nature and significance of economists' claims of knowledge about human social interaction. Most books on the philosophy of science are preoccupied with the natural sciences, especially in the twentieth century, physics. Many economics textbooks begin with a statement of the orthodox position on the status of economics as a social science. Only rarely, however, are the themes introduced in these introductory chapters revisited. Once the student is absorbed in the content of the subject matter, it apparently serves no useful purpose to confuse matters with esoteric philosophical controversies.

Mastery of the philosophy of economic science is an interdisciplinary inquiry. It requires an understanding of the structure and the content of economic reasoning as well as familiarity with ideas from the philosophy of science. Economists have not been encouraged to study philosophy since their intellectual ancestors wrestled their discipline away from departments of moral and social philosophy in the late nineteenth century. Memories of this separation continue to scar both fields. Students of philosophy are, if appearances are correct, forbidden to study economics even today. This legacy is as tragic as it is misguided.

The term 'Methodology' is used by economists to signify two quite different things. Methodology is often misused to mean method, procedure, technique, or an approach to modelling, as in 'computable general equilibrium methodology'. Methods, procedures and techniques, *per se*, are not the subject of this book. I am concerned here with the second meaning of methodology. In these pages, methodology denotes the study of the process of appraisal of theories that are purported to be scientific. Methodology is the theory of theories. It analyses the process through which knowledge about economic phenomena is authenticated. Methodology is closely related to epistemology. Epistemology is the study or the theory of the origins, the nature, the methods of authentication and the limits of knowledge. The epistemology of economics is concerned with the sources of economists' knowledge about human social interaction, the scope of application of that knowledge, and the protocol through which that knowledge is validated.

Methodologists are also concerned with semantics and, more recently, rhetoric. Methodological distinctions often hinge on the meanings that economists attach to key words. For example, concepts such as individualism, subjectivism, explanation, prediction, understanding, causation and even theory or model represent important territorial barriers between methodological doctrines in economics. Rhetorical analysis of economics, pioneered by Donald McCloskey, seeks to understand the ways in which economists try to persuade one another regarding conflicting claims of economic knowledge.

This book treats methodology as a normative enterprise. An alternative perspective sometimes referred to as the sociology of knowledge approach, emphasizes the positive aspects of methodological inquiry. It asks how economists do appraise theories rather than how they should appraise theories. Much work in positive methodology seems to have been inspired by Thomas Kuhn's *The Structure of Scientific Revolutions* (1970). Kuhn introduced some influential ideas into the lexicon of methodology. Scientific revolutions occur when one paradigm in a scientific discipline replaces another. Kuhn used the term paradigm to mean many things, but for our purposes the idea of a world view or perspective are adequate synonyms. According to Kuhn, normal science occupies most of the time and efforts of most scientists working in a field of study. Normal science consists of a shared set of priorities, models and methods to be used to address an agenda of research problems considered to lie within the scope of a particular discipline. Eventually, however, anomalies and paradoxes, problems that prove difficult to solve with the conventional paradigm, reach a critical mass and a new paradigm is proposed to accommodate these anomalies. One of Kuhn's more controversial claims is that practitioners of the new paradigm may be unable to effectively communicate with their counterparts in the old paradigm because key concepts in the new paradigm may be incommensurable with those in the old one. The three episodes described by Coase, which were discussed in Chapter 2, are an example of positive methodology. In Kuhn's terms, Coase describes three paradigm shifts or scientific revolutions. A limitation of Kuhn's model in economics is that it would seem that, in economics, old paradigms never die. In any case, this book follows the normative tradition in methodology. My goal is to survey the leading proposals that economists have made as to how theory appraisal should proceed in economics.

A TRADITIONAL VIEW OF METHODOLOGY

The product of methodological inquiry is a set of criteria for theory appraisal. These criteria help distinguish between valid theories and invalid ones.

Eichner (1983) describes three components of the process of theory appraisal (Figure 3.1): coherence, correspondence, and clarity and simplicity. Coherence is concerned with the logical integrity of a theory. Do the conclusions, predictions or hypotheses follow from the axioms or premises? Do statements in the theory contradict each other? Correspondence is concerned with the relationship between the theory and the relevant phenomena. There are at least three aspects involved in the methodological assessment of correspondence for an economic theory:

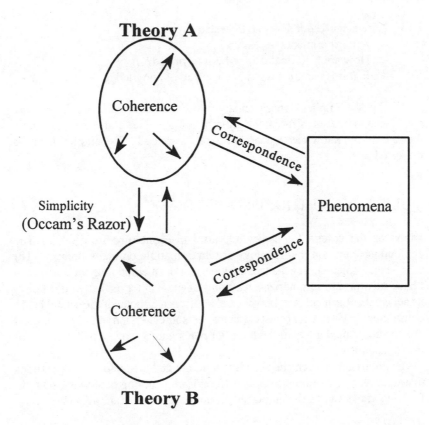

Figure 3.1   Criteria for theory appraisal

- Delineation of the scope of application of the theory
  - To what phenomena does the theory relate?
  - Under what conditions is it intended to apply?
- Identification of the elements or statements in the theory to which tests of correspondence are to be applied
  - Are all statements, including assumptions, predictions and hypotheses to be assessed or only some sub-set?

and finally,

- How is correspondence to be tested?
  - Are experiments necessary?
  - How are historical data to be interpreted?
  - Is introspection a legitimate source of knowledge?

Clarity and simplicity are secondary virtues of a theory. If two theories are considered to be equivalent on the grounds of coherence and correspondence, then a criterion known as 'Occam's Razor' is applied. The simpler theory is preferred.

QUESTIONS METHODOLOGISTS ASK

Views on the criteria for theory appraisal in economics are diverse. The contending views on methodology are incompatible on many points. The following chapters survey the leading views on the methodology of economics. I have attempted to summarize each point of view in terms that would satisfy its adherents. Each chapter, however, also offers a critique of the school being considered. Most economists adhere to some version of either logical positivism supplemented with Popper's idea of falsification or instrumentalism.

The discussion in each chapter visits fundamental methodological questions that serve as a type of litmus test in differentiating among competing schools. Existing views can be distinguished on the basis of their answers to:

1. What is the purpose of economic inquiry?
2. What are the legitimate sources of knowledge about economic phenomena?
3. What is the scope of the subject matter of economics? What are the limits to the application of that knowledge? and
4. What is the appropriate structure of economic theories or models?

In addition, methodological doctrines draw distinctions regarding the meaning and significance of technical terms. Ideas such as rationality and equilibrium as well as notions such as prediction, explanation and understanding are all important in differentiating among points of view.

What is the Purpose of Economic Analysis?

This is arguably the most fundamental methodological question. Evaluation implies a standard. Theory appraisal is blind without an idea of what theorizing should accomplish.

Almost all economists are concerned about the 'policy implications' of their work. These implications may be related to individual behaviour, to the actions of organizations, or to political actions. Even a conclusion that the government should *not* do something, such as employing protectionist measures to interfere with the international flow of commodities, is a policy implication. This interest in implications indicates an overarching purpose for economic analysis beyond the satisfaction of intellectual curiosity. Economists seek to enhance the general level of welfare of people. They seek to facilitate peaceful coordinated social interaction among their fellow human beings. This aim is rarely stated explicitly, but without it, most of the things that economists do cannot be rationalized. This goal is widely misconstrued to represent an exclusive concern with material or financial wellbeing, and this misunderstanding has created much mischief.

While economists are almost universally committed to the goal of enhancing the general level of human welfare, they are deeply divided on the question of how to best pursue this vision. The controversy relates to what I will call instrumental purposes. An instrumental purpose is a strategy for achieving some ultimate goal. There are two principal competing views.[1] According to one tradition, successful economic inquiry makes it possible to understand social phenomena. Armed with this understanding, we are better equipped to apprehend the consequences of intentionally changing social institutions. Much of the prescriptive advice is cautionary. This tradition emphasizes what we might call qualitative rather than quantitative analysis and prediction. Some writers working in this tradition, such as Hayek, talk about pattern prediction as the product of understanding. This is differentiated from outcome prediction.

A second tradition sees the instrumental purpose of economic analysis as explanation. In economics, explanation usually follows the 'Covering Law' model. According to the covering law model, explanation consists of showing that a particular situation is an example of a general principle or 'covering law'. For example, an apple falling from a tree is an instance of the force of gravity. In economics, explanation generally involves the demonstration that a particular situation could be the product of interaction among rational individuals.[2] Several notions of rationality have been employed in economic explanations including utility maximization, profit maximization, expected utility maximization, and present value maximization.

The explanation tradition emphasizes measurement, quantitative prediction and control of social phenomena. It stresses the importance of quantitative analysis and statistical hypothesis testing based on the principle of rationality. Predictions derived from rationality explanations are outcome predictions. They lend themselves to quantitative measurement and testing.

These two instrumental purposes are not the same. They imply different criteria for the measurement of progress. They require different approaches to scholarship and anticipate different content to the evolution of knowledge.

Examples of the purposes of economic inquiry

Almost every economics textbook begins with a statement such as 'The purpose of economics is ...'. This tradition might be puzzling to a chemist or a zoologist. This preoccupation with the goal of a discipline is uncommon in the natural sciences. Economists have offered many versions of the purpose of economic inquiry. Figure 3.2 lists nine purposes of economic inquiry that have been advocated by economists from time to time. After more than 200 years, the purpose of economic inquiry is not yet a closed question. For example, Henderson and Quandt (1980, p. 1) maintain that 'Explanation and prediction are the goals of economics as well as most other sciences'. According to Henderson and Quandt, theories are deductive, drawing conclusions from a set of initial assumptions. Empirical work in economics employs inductive reasoning. These two types of reasoning are seen as complementary, but the nature of the relationship between theory and observation is not explained. They do state that the proper scope of empirical study includes assessment of the degree to which the assumptions as well as the conclusions of theories correspond to observations. They go on to say, however, that 'the requirement of a strict conformity between theory and fact would defeat the very purpose of theory. Theories represent simplifications and generalizations of reality and therefore do not completely describe particular situations ... increased understanding is realized at the cost of the sacrificed detail.'

To Gary Becker (1976), the purpose of economic theory is to provide a comprehensive framework for the study of human behaviour. The 'economic approach' to the study of human behaviour consists of three elements: a notion of human rationality expressed as utility maximization, stable and identical preferences and markets that are generally in equilibrium. The framework provided by economic theory requires knowledge from other disciplines to be useful in a particular context. Its utility derives from its ability to provide a consistent explanation of human behaviour in a variety of seemingly unrelated contexts. Economic analysis helps make sense of a complex reality.

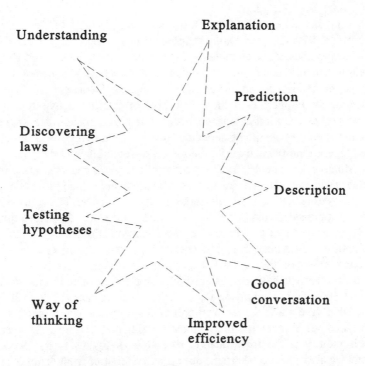

Understanding

Explanation

Prediction

Discovering laws

Testing hypotheses

Description

Way of thinking

Improved efficiency

Good conversation

Figure 3.2 The purposes of economic inquiry

Fritz Machlup (1978) also considered explanation to be the purpose of economic theory, but he was more circumspect about the limits of economic explanation. Reviewing the heated exchange about the realism of assumptions in the neoclassical theory of the firm during the 1930s and 1940s (see Lester, 1946, 1947 and Friedman 1953), Machlup concluded that there are four possible purposes of price theory. In principle, microeconomic theory could furnish answers to four types of questions:

1. What will the prices of cotton textiles be?
2. What prices will the X corporation charge?
3. How will the prices of cotton textiles be affected by an increase in wages?
4. How will the X corporation change its prices when wage rates are increased?

Machlup argued that price theory was only intended to answer questions like (3). In his words 'The model of the theory of the firm ... is designed to explain and predict changes in observed prices ... as effects of particular changes in conditions. ... This is altogether different from explaining the behaviour of a firm' (Machlup, 1978, p. 399).

To Paul Samuelson (1947/1979), Mark Blaug (1980, 1992) and Eugene Silberberg (1979, Chapter 1), the purpose of economic theory is to produce refutable hypotheses. A refutable hypothesis is a statement, derived from the axioms of a theory, that could be falsified by observation. This position on the purpose of theory is based on Karl Popper's Demarcation Criterion. According to Popper, it is the generation of falsifiable hypotheses that separates science from non-science. Consequently, if economists want to be scientific, then they should be about the business of deriving what Samuelson called 'operationally meaningful theorems' or refutable hypotheses.

To Milton Friedman (1953), the purpose of economic analysis is to produce reliable predictions. In fact Friedman's influential and still controversial essay states that this is the singular purpose of economic theory. The sole criterion in theory appraisal should be predictive success. Friedman dismissed the idea that economic theories should be assessed on the accuracy of their assumptions. This position, while continuing to be controversial, has had a profound impact on the conduct of economic research.

Other economists have emphasized the contribution of economic theory to the understanding of human social interaction. Karl Popper (1989, p. 342) has argued that, 'the main task of the theoretical social sciences ... is to trace the unintended social repercussions of intentional human actions'. The product of this inquiry is the identification of social analogues to the ways that technological knowledge sharpens our understanding of what is not possible. Just as 'The second law of thermodynamics can be expressed as the technological warning, "You cannot build a machine that is 100 percent efficient." A similar rule of the social sciences would be, "You cannot, without increasing productivity, raise the real income of the working population."' According to Henry Hazlitt (1979, p. 17), 'The art of economics consists in looking not merely at the immediate but at the longer effects of any act or policy; it consists in tracing the consequences of that policy not merely for one group but for all groups'. This art is closely related to Hayek's (1973, p. 37) claim that 'It would be no exaggeration to say that social theory begins with – and has an object only because of – the discovery that there exist orderly structures which were the product of the action of many men but are not the result of human design'. Hayek goes on to argue that the purpose of economic theory is to facilitate understanding regarding the existence and the character of the orderly structures that arise out of voluntary exchange relations among people. Making the point even more strongly, Walter Block (1986, pp. 57–58) claims it is probably only a slight exaggeration to say that the main and indeed the only task of the instructor of economics is to teach his beginning students precisely this lesson (to be able to see competition as a form of social cooperation). If the professor succeeds, he will have imparted a good grounding in his subject to his charges, even if that is the only thing he does. If he fails in this one goal, his students will still be economically illiterate, no matter to what other exotica they may have been introduced.

James Buchanan (1964) also emphasizes the potential contribution of economic analysis to understanding, but he argues that this potential has not been realized. By following Lionel Robbins' definition of economics as the study of resource allocation under conditions of scarcity, Buchanan claims that economists have limited the ability of economic theory to foster understanding of the character of voluntary exchange relations. He prefers Adam Smith's description of economics as the study of the human propensity to truck, barter and exchange. Economic theory ought to enable us to better apprehend the nature of social coordination through voluntary exchange relations.

Robert Heilbronner (1980) is another advocate of understanding as the aim of economic inquiry, although his perspective often differs from that of Hayek, Block, Hazlett and Buchanan. According to the Classical Marxist tradition, the aim of economic theory is 'the identification and explication of hidden problems in society's process of material self-reproduction'.

Ludwig von Mises (1981) maintained that the purpose of economic inquiry was to discover and articulate the universal laws of human social interaction that emerge through voluntary exchange relations among self-interested individuals in a free society. Mises emphasized the importance of understanding in his exposition of those laws. An adequate understanding of the price system, according to Mises, contributes to a reluctance to interfere with that system to achieve political goals.

Finally, this brief survey would be incomplete if it did not acknowledge the role of economic theory in the criticism of government policy. Worswick (1972) states that 'There are few contemporary economists who would not claim that their work and their ideas are intended to contribute in some degree, however indirectly, to the improvement of a firm, or an industry, or a national economy or the world as a whole' (Worswick, 1972, p. 76). With characteristic candour, Mises (1966, p. 67) puts it this way.

> It is impossible to understand the history of economic thought if one does not pay attention to the fact that economics as such is a challenge to the conceit of those in power. An economist can never be the favourite of autocrats and demagogues. With them, he is always the mischief maker, and the more they are inwardly convinced that his objections are well founded, the more they hate him.

The purpose of economic analysis is a watershed methodological issue. Exponents of different schools can often be differentiated on the basis of their answer to this question. Sometimes, the differentiation is based on the relative weight attached to the various purposes of economics. Many views on the purpose of economics beg deeper questions of meaning. What constitutes a prediction? Is a prediction an unconditional forecast, or is it contingent? Is a prediction necessarily quantitative or can it be qualitative? What does it mean to understand or to explain some social phenomenon using economic theory? I will return to these themes in later chapters.

What is the Source or Origin of Economic Knowledge?

There are potentially four sources of economic knowledge (Figure 3.3). Knowledge may originate from extra-human entities (Revelation), it may originate in self-knowledge (Reason) or introspection, it may originate in objective human observation of the external world (Observation), or it may originate in tradition. The debate over the relative merits of reason and observation is one of the enduring controversies in the philosophy of science. It has implications for methodological disputes in economics as well.

Extra-human entities are not seen as an important source of economic knowledge by most economists today but this was not always the case. The scholastics theory of the just price was an attempt to derive an economic theory from revelational writings. Medieval proscriptions against lending money at interest were an attempt to derive an economic policy based on revelational sources. More recently, some writers have advanced the notion of the 'intrinsic value' of the natural world. This category of value is described as independent of human perceptions or use. A theory of intrinsic value appeals to knowledge about values residing outside the human race and thus represents an extra-human source of economic knowledge. With a few exceptions, however, economists have abandoned the idea that economic knowledge can originate outside human consciousness.

Some economists all of the time and almost all economists some of the time accept introspection as a source of economic knowledge. The idea here is that the economist, by examining his or her own motives, perceptions and actions can gain general insights about patterns of human social interaction. Introspection is closely linked to the various notions of rationality employed by economists. The appropriate role of introspection and the status of knowledge obtained through this practice continue to be contentious methodological issues among economists.

The third source of economic knowledge is observation. Some methodological doctrines in economics maintain that observation is the only source of scientific economic knowledge. Observation in economics involves the measurement of historical values of prices or of quantities of commodities and factors of production. The subdiscipline of econometrics has emerged as the branch of economics which seeks to interpret and analyse historical data.

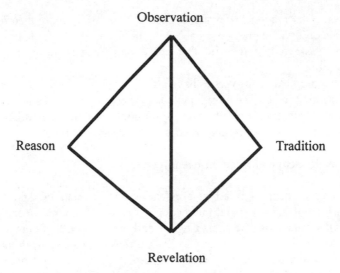

Figure 3.3 Sources of knowledge in economic inquiry

The contribution of tradition as a source of knowledge has been best explained by Popper (1989, Introduction). Popper's ideas on this subject will be explained in Chapter 4.

Methodologists are not only concerned with general questions about the admissible sources of knowledge about economic phenomena. They are also interested in how knowledge from each potential source should be authenticated. For extra-human sources of knowledge, methodologists want to know how humans can assess the authority of the extra-human source. For introspection, they want to know how the self-knowledge of a particular individual can be extended to general propositions about other people. They also might like to know how to resolve conflicts among competing introspections. The logical positivists sought to establish foundations for scientific knowledge exclusively from observation. This programme was undertaken in an attempt to purge scientific discourse of metaphysical statements as well as ideology and subjectivism. A methodology of science, however, that admits only observation as a legitimate source of knowledge, stumbles on the problem of induction. How can observation *prove* the validity of a theory? Perhaps a sequence of observed confirmations are merely the product of coincidence. An empiricist methodology must also resolve the problem of theory dependence. Theory dependence arises when the conceptual framework used by a researcher conditions the questions asked and the observations made in research. Do the theoretical categories of the researcher create an obstacle to objectivity? Or do they prevent him or her from noticing phenomena that have no representation in theory? Finally, the problem of observational equivalence creates a conundrum for theory selection. Observational equivalence occurs when two or more theories make the same observable predictions about phenomena. How should economists choose between two theories that are equally consistent with available observations?

Methodological controversies have also flourished over the relevant focus of efforts to observe. The most infamous of these controversies in economics involved the empirical validation of assumptions. Should economists attempt to determine if the assumptions used in a theory are accurate?

What is the Scope of Economic Analysis?

Is economic theory limited in application to the material and financial dimensions of human social interaction? Or can economic theory provide insight into situations where less tangible ends are the object of human action? Adam Smith, J. Neville Keynes and J.E. Cairnes used a narrow definition of economics, at least by contemporary standards. They viewed their subject as the study of the laws that determine the level of material wellbeing in a society. Beginning with Lionel Robbins (1932), economists have increasingly expanded the boundaries of their discipline to encompass more and more facets of human behaviour. Gary Becker's work in the economics of education and the family are well known, but the economists' notions of rationality and equilibrium have also been used by legal theorists (Coleman, 1992), by students of politics (Buchanan and Tullock, 1962, and Mueller, 1989) and by political philosophers (Gauthier, 1985). Even in biology (Oster and Wilson, 1978, and May, 1973, ref. in Rosenberg, 1992) the economists' approach of game theory has yielded fruit.

Other economists have argued that there are limits to the application of economic analysis. Some, following Frank Knight, have limited the scope of application of economics to the rational realm. Rational behaviour occurs in the context of known ends and means. The use of those known means is 'rationalized' with respect to their contribution to the advancement of the known ends. But Knight (1921), McKenzie (1983) and Kirzner (1973, 1985) in their work on entrepreneurship, have concluded that much human behaviour involves the discovery of both means and ends. This behaviour lies, by definition, outside the rational.

The limits of knowledge are defined by the scope of application of that knowledge, but also by its reliability. Most scientific disciplines have developed criteria to assess the reliability or validity of knowledge claims. The ability of other researchers to replicate results is commonly employed as an indicator of the credibility of knowledge claims. Oddly enough, this criterion has rarely been applied in economic research, and with less than complete success (see Chapter 4). Successful prediction in new areas and increased ability to control phenomena are also used as standards for assessing the credibility of knowledge claims in the natural sciences. Technological exploitation of scientific discoveries from medical research and research in the physical sciences are often used to justify research budgets. If the technology works as advertised, presumably the scientific knowledge claims on which it is based must have some reliability.

Application of these standards in economics has been problematical. Replication of empirical results may mean replication with the same data. This constitutes a check on computation and accuracy in reporting. Empirical replication with different data would require a constancy in the estimated relationships or parameters that transcended time, institutions or location. Some cases of replication in measurement have been achieved. Estimates of the own price elasticity of demand for milk invariably find that consumption is not very responsive to price. Replication in hypothesis testing has been more difficult to achieve (see Fox and Kivanda, 1994, and Cozzarin and Gilmour, forthcoming).

The 'technology' analogy is also difficult to apply. Adoption of the findings of economic research usually requires cooperation in the political realm. Public choice theory has furnished a long list of reasons for believing that this cooperation might be in short supply. Does half-hearted adoption of a policy, leading to a failure to realize the conditions anticipated by the economist, constitute a refutation of that economist's claim of knowledge about economic phenomena?

Finally, economists, in a very broad sense, are students of human behaviour. They are participant observers, and their subject matter can learn and adapt to changing information, including economic knowledge obtained through economic research. That increased knowledge can change the very behaviour of the subjects under study. What does this do for replication and application? It is conceivable that economic knowledge may carry the seeds of its own obsolescence.

What is the Appropriate Structure of a Scientific Theory?

The most general structural question in the methodology of economics has to do with the extent to which economics is like other branches of science. Should the criteria for theory appraisal in economics resemble those in the physical or biological sciences? It turns out that there are two positions on this question: Yes and No. The yes view, often described as Monism, contends that the principles of theory appraisal are common to all scientific disciplines. Only subject matter differentiates branches of science.

Those who answer this question in the negative argue that theory appraisal should differ across scientific disciplines. Dualists maintain that disciplines which study human behaviour need a fundamentally different logic of theory appraisal from those that do not. Pluralists argue that even this fragmentation does not go far enough in that it does not adequately accommodate the differences between experimental and non-experimental natural sciences.

Other structural controversies relate more to the content of economic theories. Much of economic theory conforms to the structural description of Becker (1976) and Weintraub (1985), that rational action is synonymous with constrained optimization, that choices are animated by preferences and expectations, and that voluntary exchange in markets creates and sustains equilibrium in those markets.

Nearly all economists characterize human behaviour as 'rational', in one sense or another. In some circles, rationality means the maximization of a continuous twice differentiable quasi-concave utility function subject to a budget constraint or a resource endowment. Elsewhere, rationality means only purposeful action. Rationality is considered by some to be partial, either in the sense that it is only pursued so far, as in satisficing behaviour, or in the sense that it is only pursued in some subset of human endeavours. So while there is broad agreement on the structure of economic theory being based on rational human action, there is considerable disagreement on what rationality means.

The notion of equilibrium is widely used in economic theory, but in fundamentally different ways. To some, perpetual and pervasive equilibrium is a description of market relations in the world around us. Lack of equilibrium is symptomatic of someone not acting on the opportunity to get something for nothing. If nature abhors a vacuum, economists abhor the prospect of something for nothing. But other economists see equilibration as a tendency that is ever present, but nearly always thwarted by technological innovation, natural resource discoveries and changes in preferences.

Finally, the role of mathematics in economic inquiry is an ongoing source of tension. Is mathematical expression *necessary* for the statement of knowledge claims in economics? Are there more and less fruitful uses of mathematics in economic analysis?

GENERAL PROBLEMS IN THE PHILOSOPHY OF SOCIAL SCIENCE

Social scientists continue to be divided on methodological questions. These classical controversies have periodically been important in economics. As I mentioned earlier, economists do not yet agree whether the purpose of their subject is understanding or explanation and predication. This question has also divided practitioners of other social sciences (see Hollis, 1994).

A second point of traditional tension has surrounded the question of whether the social sciences should proceed along holistic or individualistic lines. In this context, individualism means that either explanation or understanding of social phenomena can only be considered to be complete when it has been explicitly linked to the purposes, perceptions and actions of individuals. Social phenomena, in a sense, are only the sum of their parts, those parts being individual actions. Holism views phenomena at a more aggregate level than individual choice as having a life of their own. Economists generally follow an individualist bent, however, Keynesian macroeconomic theory with its aggregate consumption function and the notion of the fallacy of composition are important exceptions.

A third traditional tension is between rationalism and empiricism. This is an ancient controversy going back at least to Bacon. Is knowledge to be grounded exclusively in the senses, in observation? Or is reason, logic, introspection and intuition the ultimate source of knowledge? Orthodoxy in economic methodology is empiricist, but the actual practice of economists is often closet rationalism.

Finally, there has been disagreement among philosophers of science[3] as to whether theories should be judged on the basis of their truthfulness or their usefulness. The instrumentalists, as the name suggests, argued that theories are only instruments. They should be judged on the basis of whether they are useful or not. Truth, according to this view, is beyond the apprehension of mere mortals. If a theory predicts well, and this is the sense in which the word useful is used, then that is the best that we can hope for.

CHARACTERISTIC PROBLEMS OF SCIENTIFIC ECONOMICS

The subject matter of economic research creates some vexing problems for practitioners of a discipline that aspires to be known as scientific. First, economic data are historical. Since these data were produced without the benefit of controlled experiments, they face the very problems of interpretation that experiments were created to solve. Experiments are conducted to isolate mechanisms and effects. Given the ethical and practical barriers to the use of the experimental approach in economic research, economists face formidable problems of confounding in their data sets. If the price of corn rises and at the same time the price of fertilizer falls and interest rates also decline, what share of the observed increase in corn production should be attributed to the influence of each factor? And how much is a result of the weather? Economists have devoted an enormous effort to combating problems of confounding and collinearity in historical data, especially with the rise in importance of econometrics in the postwar era, but available data are often not rich enough to enable economists to distinguish between observationally equivalent theories. Of course this problem is not unique to economics. Astronomers, meteorologists, epidemiologists as well as social scientists in anthropology and sociology are also frequently unable to conduct experiments.

A second problematic aspect of the subject matter of economics has to do with the diversity of human beings. People have different goals, preferences, perceptions, expectations and abilities. On top of that, environmental factors such as life experiences, cultural traditions and social institutions vary widely.

Economics, however, seeks understanding of human social interaction that transcends time and place. Economists do not wish to produce an economic theory of seventeenth century French agriculture or an economic theory of twentieth century Chinese manufacturing. Economic theory is intended to yield insights in both of these contexts and in a wide range of other situations.

Dissension over values has plagued economics since its inception. Economics is a branch of the study of human behaviour, especially human behaviour in a social context. Even though twentieth century economists have struggled valiantly to produce a value-free science of economics, it has proved difficult if not impossible to lay aside ethical ideals about human society while theorizing about that society. Ethical ideals influence the perception and diagnosis of problems for research. To some, inequality in the distribution of income or wealth is an amoral artifact of free and consensual human interaction. To others, an unequal distribution of income is a problem that needs to be corrected. Instability in market prices also has a dual interpretation. To some, price movements signify an important source of information about social change. To others, price movements are a source of discomfort and disruption that should be moderated or eliminated. What is a problem to one analyst can be a solution to another.

Economics has been accused of disciplinary imperialism, as inroads into law, political studies, the family, ethics, constitutional design and anthropology have occurred. Economists' notions of rationality have proved powerful at explicating diverse areas of human behaviour. This broadening of horizons has not been achieved without cost, however. Expanding boundaries of the discipline require more and more integration of economic theory with social theory generally. As Cordato (1992) has recently emphasized, even a theory of market exchange requires a foundational theory of just ownership. And a theory of just ownership is just one element in a general theory of ethics. A theory of government policy, say as a response to market failure or macroeconomic instability, requires a theory of the political process, which may, in turn, invoke a normative theory of the state. The traditional perception of science sees the process of discovery as reductionist. The goal is to isolate mechanisms and processes into more and more fundamental constituent elements. The evolution of economics as a body of knowledge seems to belie that traditional understanding, if economics is accepted in the community of scientific disciplines.

WHY BOTHER WITH METHODOLOGY?

George Stigler once said that economists should be forbidden from studying, talking about or writing about methodology until they are at least 65 years of age. This opinion seems to be shared by many economists, at least if the design of undergraduate and graduate curricula is any indication. Few departments of economics or agricultural economics offer courses in the subject. Most philosophy departments ignore the peculiar problems of the methodology of economics in their offerings in the philosophy of science. But this state of affairs is changing. As Chapter 1 indicated, the literature on the methodology of economics has virtually exploded in the last twenty years. What is the impetus behind this development? The most ready explanation is the collapse of macroeconomics as a body of knowledge. Macroeconomics has been one of the most visible fields of economics in this century. It would be difficult to overestimate its influence on public policy. Its recent balkanization into isolated factions has likely been a key factor contributing to the recent rebirth of interest in the methodology of economics.

James Buchanan, in his insightful essay 'What Should Economists Do?' (1964) made a cogent case for the study of economic methodology as part of the necessary preparation for a research career. He argued that a knowledge of methodology is like a roadmap. He acknowledges that the metaphor is not completely accurate in that the reason that research is needed in any field is that the information required to draw a 'roadmap' is not available! Nevertheless, Buchanan suggests that the process of selection of problems for research can be better undertaken with a familiarity of the principles of the philosophy of science in general and of the methodology of economics in particular.

J. Neville Keynes, J.E. Cairnes and Ludwig von Mises, in different ways, suggested another reason why economists need to master the methodology of their subject. They all insisted that economics is inherently political. Its principles often define limits of political action. As a consequence, the authority of those principles is sure to be challenged by those who object to the constraints that those principles impose. According to this view, the twentieth century pursuit of a value-free scientific economics is a fool's errand. Economics and ethics and values are inseparable. It behoves the economist, therefore, to understand the basis and the limits of the knowledge claims that his or her discipline makes.

Economics is more than conversation. It is more than academic puzzle solving. People make decisions based on their understanding of economic principles. When these people are making decisions about government policy, large numbers of people can potentially be affected. These people may lose their jobs, see the value of their savings rise or fall, they may face new opportunities, or they may have to move. If the collectivization of Russian and Chinese agriculture is seen as the product of decisions made with defective economic theory, then those theoretical defects cost millions of people their lives. It is precisely the need to differentiate between authentic and non-authentic claims to economic knowledge that undergirds the importance of the methodology of economics.

QUESTIONS FOR DISCUSSION

1. Explain the distinctions between explanation and understanding.
2. Do you think that the study of methodology is important in the education of an economist?
3. What do you think is the purpose of economic inquiry?
4. How has the definition of economics changed over the last 200 years?
5. Can economics follow the same rules for theory appraisal as the natural sciences, or does it need its own criteria?

NOTES

1. I have elected to describe these two views as understanding and explanation, based on Hollis (1994). Understanding involves appreciating the nature and meaning of a situation from an insider's perspective. Explanation involves interpreting a situation as an example of a general class of phenomena. According to this distinction, explanation is closely related to prediction and often to control. Some economic methodologists (for example, Lawson, 1992) characterize these two contending views, respectively, as explanation versus prediction. I find Hollis's categories more illuminating of differences among contending schools of thought in economic methodology.
2. There are some exceptions to this individualism. Classical Marxists explain in terms of the inevitable dynamics implied by the reproduction of the means of production.
3. And among philosophical scientists.

4. Economics as Positivism and Falsificationism

INTRODUCTION

The orthodox view on economic methodology is a combination of ideas from logical positivism supplemented with the demarcation criterion of Sir Karl Popper.[1] The hallmark of this orthodoxy is a concern over testable, refutable or falsifiable hypotheses. Contemporary advocates of economics as falsification include Terence Hutchison (1938), Paul Samuelson (1947/1979), Mark Blaug and Eugene Silberberg (1979). Blaug's *The Methodology of Economics* (1980, 1992) is the most unequivocal and passionate statement of falsificationism in the economics literature.

Terence Hutchison's *The Significance and Basic Postulates of Economic Theory* (1938) introduced positivist Popperian methodology to economics. Hutchison rejected the *a priorism*[2] of Lionel Robbins, and therefore, indirectly, of Nassau Senior, John Neville Keynes, J.E. Cairnes and Ludwig von Mises. He presents Popper's demarcation criterion in English and in terms that were familiar to economists. Popper's *The Logic of Scientific Discovery* was published in German in 1935, but did not appear in an English translation until 1959. Hutchison's acknowledgement of Popper is obscure, but the influence of Popper's ideas is unmistakable.

Even before Hutchison's book, however, the ideas of positivism were beginning to influence the thinking of economists on methodology. The creation of the Econometric Society showed a profoundly positivist slant. The inaugural issue of *Econometrica*,[3] contains a statement of the editorial policy of the new journal, the Constitution of the society and an important paper by Joseph Schumpeter. All three show strong positivist inclinations. They affirm the unity of science doctrine. The aim of the society was to advance economic theory through the use of mathematics and statistics and the empirical and quantitative approach employed in the natural sciences. The activities of the society were not intended to advance any ideology nor are its members interested in, according to Schumpeter, raising any debate regarding method. Schumpeter took it as self evident that all of the great economists displayed a 'mathematical bent'.

51

Paul Samuelson's (1947/1979) *Foundations* begins with a methodological chapter that further clarifies the positivist research programme. According to Samuelson, the purpose of economic theory is to produce what he called 'operationally meaningful theorems'. These are defined as hypotheses 'about empirical data which could conceivably be refuted'. These hypotheses are not arbitrary. They are deduced from the structure of a mathematical optimization problem. The terms used in the discussion differ from Popper and Hutchison but the intent is the same.

Sir Karl Popper's notion of falsification has had a deep and abiding impact on the methodological views of economists. Popper saw himself as a critic of logical positivism. The thrust of his criticism was aimed at early positivists' emphasis on confirmation as the test of correspondence of a theory. Popper argued that confirmation was too easy. Finding evidence to confirm a theory did not constitute a rigorous test. He also contended that confirmation did not resolve the problem of induction. As an alternative, Popper suggested falsification as a more demanding standard for testing correspondence. A refutable or testable or falsifiable hypothesis is a statement that could, at least conceivably, be contradicted by observation. The special status of the falsifiable hypothesis derives from Sir Karl Popper's demarcation criterion. According to Popper, the distinction between science and non-science is that science produces and tests refutable hypotheses and non-science does not. Scientific knowledge consists of the set of refutable hypotheses which have not yet been falsified.

If Popper saw himself as a dissenter from logical positivism, the distinction between his position and his adversaries has often been lost on economists. Falsification has been grafted on to the root of logical positivism in orthodox economic methodology. The result is an empiricist or positivist position with a falsificationist standard for testing correspondence.

LOGICAL POSITIVISM AND THE FOUR KEY METHODOLOGICAL QUESTIONS

What is the Purpose of Economic Analysis?

According to the mainstream view, the purpose of economic analysis is to generate and test refutable hypotheses. Economists, presumably, would like to be seen as scientists. They should therefore aspire to develop theories that are falsifiable. According to Mark Blaug, economists either universally embrace falsification as the crucial element of theory appraisal, or they should. He is critical of the shallowness of economists' commitment to falsificationism, however. In his words, 'Modern economists frequently preach falsificationism, but they rarely practice it' (1980, p. 128). In fact, 'the central weakness of modern economics is ... the reluctance to produce theories that yield unambiguously refutable implications followed by a general unwillingness to confront those implications with the facts' (1980, p. 254). But Blaug is unwavering in his insistence that falsificationism is the appropriate methodological doctrine in economics. The problem lies with the profligacy of economists.

What is the Source of Economic Knowledge?

Logical positivism stakes a bold and unequivocal claim about the legitimate source of economic knowledge. The exclusive legitimate source of scientific knowledge in economics is observation. Logical positivism was developed by a group that came to be known as the Vienna Circle. It consisted of a group of philosophically-oriented scientists affiliated with the University of Vienna in the 1920s. Their aim was the elimination of metaphysics from scientific discourse and the creation of an objective basis for scientific knowledge. Metaphysics in this context means beyond or transcending the physical. In practice, the elimination of metaphysics was an attempt to remove introspection and reason from the list of admissible sources of scientific knowledge.

The Vienna Circle rejected the use of speculation about the nature of reality as part of scientific inquiry. The use of introspection and reflection and reasoning based on these sources was considered unscientific. Speculation, in their view, introduced subjectivity and ideology into scientific inquiry. To the members of the circle, knowledge claims about the external world could only be validated by experience. Experience meant objective experience, that is, observation and not introspection. Science consists of the logical analysis of empirical phenomena. Early versions of positivism emphasized verification or confirmation as the appropriate process for validating knowledge claims.

The logical positivists drew part of their inspiration from Kant's distinction between analytic and synthetic statements.[4] An analytic statement is a logical statement in the sense that its truthfulness can be assessed exclusively through the methods of deductive logic. Analytic statements are true in all possible worlds, independently of facts or observation. They are true by virtue of definitions alone. Positivists often refer to such statements as tautological. Technically, tautological signifies true by definition in an obvious way, bordering on redundant. To the logical positivists, the term signified a statement 'without meaning'. It did not convey knowledge about the external world.

Synthetic statements are simply statements that are not analytic. Under logical positivism, they take on an additional significance. Only synthetic statements can be meaningful. Only synthetic statements can convey knowledge about the external world. While analytic statements may be true, they cannot, by definition, be meaningful. Meaningfulness is the highest category in a positivist hierarchy.

A posteriori and *a priori* statements are closely related concepts. *A posteriori* statements can only be determined to be true or false through experience or observation. *A priori* statements are proved true or false exclusively through reason. Reasoning proceeds from propositions whose truth is accepted as self-evident or as necessary for experience to be intelligible.

Any empiricist methodological doctrine, and especially an empiricist doctrine that admits only observation as the source of meaningful knowledge, needs to resolve the problem of induction. The problem of induction arises when we want to prove something by appealing to observation. Even a long sequence of observed confirmations, according to Hume, does not constitute proof. This sequence of confirmations may be the product of coincidence. To use a famous example, 100 observations of white swans does not constitute proof that all swans are white. Nor would 1000 observations suffice. The same swan may have been observed more than once. Maybe non-white swans exist but the observer has not been observing in the area where they are located. Or perhaps the observer was preceded by hunters who shot all the non-white swans. The point is that there is a logical leap involved between the statement that 'We have observed X 100 times' and 'X is a universal law'. The second statement is a general claim about the true nature of phenomena. It is a universal statement that implies a prediction. X will always happen under a specified set of circumstances. The first statement is a summary of a sequence of particular statements about particular events that fails to contradict a general statement about phenomena.

Popper introduced the demarcation criterion in an attempt to solve the problem of induction. He argued that confirmation was too easy and subject to abuse. And even under ideal circumstances, even a long sequence of confirmations could founder on Hume's induction problem. Inductive proof is not possible. No finite number of confirming observations constitutes proof. On the other hand, a single contrary observation could falsify a universal statement. The observation of a single black swan, a single particular statement, falsifies the universal statement 'All swans are white'.

Popper exploited this asymmetry in the proof of falsehood relative to proof of truth in his definition of the boundaries of scientific inquiry. His definition also produced practical consequences for the conduct of scientific research. Science includes all human activities that generate potentially falsifiable hypotheses. A falsifiable hypothesis is a statement that is derived from the axioms of a theory or model that would be inconsistent with some observable event.

Although the following examples probably do not meet the requirement of being derived from a theory or model, they do illustrate the notion of falsifiability. The statement 'The world will end on 15 January 2006' is a falsifiable statement. If the world still exists on the morning of 16 January, the statement has been contradicted by an observable event. On the other hand, the statement 'The world will come to an end eventually' is not falsifiable. No observable event contradicts this statement. If we wake up on any particular morning and see that the world still exists, that does not contradict the statement that the world will end eventually. Falsifiable statements set unequivocal conditions that cannot occur unless the statement is false. Falsifiable statements are risky and vulnerable.

Popper recognized the problems in actually observing falsifying instances. This accounts for his use of the qualifiers, *potentially* or *conceivably* falsifiable. For an activity to qualify as scientific, it had to make potentially falsifiable statements about the phenomena that constituted its subject matter. This definition has implications for the conduct of science. Scientists work hard to derive falsifiable statements. This derivation is often difficult. Having derived hypotheses that are potentially falsifiable, however, the scientist then deliberately and painstakingly proceeds to look for falsifying observations. After having been subjected to rigorous and harsh attempts at falsification, if the hypothesis has not been contradicted by the facts, it is provisionally admitted into the class of unfalsified hypotheses. The accumulated set of not-yet-falsified hypotheses constitutes the inventory of scientific knowledge claims in a field of study.

What is the Scope of Economic Analysis?

Neither logical positivism nor Popper's notion of falsification have much to say about the boundaries of economics. This is a consequence, in part, of the unity of science doctrine of logical positivism. If the logic of theory appraisal is essentially the same for all branches of science, then boundaries between specific disciplines merely delineate categories of subject matter. These boundaries can be expected to change as knowledge advances. New discoveries may reveal similarities in phenomena previously thought to be unrelated. This development is of little consequence, as previously independent fields are integrated or abandoned in the light of the advance of knowledge.

What is the Appropriate Structure of a Scientific Theory?

Logical positivists believe that all scientific disciplines are subject to the same general rules for theory appraisal. Positivism is committed to a unity of science view. It is subject matter and not methodological principle that distinguishes scientific disciplines.

We are indebted to Eugene Silberberg (1979) for his clear description of the structural characteristics of economic theories and for his exposition of the positivist approach to the authentication of theory.[5] Economic theories consist of three elements. The core of a theory is a set of general abstract statements. These are statements about the properties of the objects to be analysed. These general statements are called postulates. They are universal statements of the form 'All X have the property P'. An example of such a postulate is 'Firms maximize profits'.

The identity and nature of the real world objects that are represented by the postulates in a theory is indeterminate at this stage. The description of the properties of these objects is not directly testable (Silberberg, 1978, p. 9). Behavioural postulates are universal statements about abstract concepts. Until the identity of these abstract entities is clearly established, they are unobservable. The testing of postulates proceeds indirectly using the other two elements of a theory, the test conditions and the hypotheses or predictions.

The test conditions, or what Silberberg calls assumptions, describe the conditions under which the theory is applicable. These assumptions must be observable and realistic. They must identify the specific real world objects to which concepts in the theory relate. They must also describe the observable conditions under which the theory is supposed to be valid. The accuracy of these assumptions is to be assessed in essentialist terms. That is, they capture the essence of the phenomena in question. According to Silberberg, 'it is impossible to describe, in a finite amount of time and space, every attribute of a given real object' (p. 8).

The third element in a theory, the predictions, is a set of unequivocal statements about situations that would not be observed if the theory were correct. Failure to observe these conditions is a failure to falsify the theory. It is not *proof* of the theory. Other theories may make predictions that have the same observable consequences. Only economic theories that make falsifiable predictions are useful. Such predictions or hypotheses must take the form that event E will occur and it must be possible to observe event E not occurring. The remainder of Silberberg's book demonstrates 'how such refutable hypotheses are derived from behavioural postulates in economics' (p. 10).

THE TRACK RECORD OF FALSIFICATIONISM

Blaug (1980, 1992) has criticized the methodological practice of economists on two grounds. He has accused them of reluctance to produce theories with refutable implications. He has also been critical of their reticence to expose theories to the possibility of contradiction. He identifies general equilibrium theory, welfare economics, international trade theory and growth theory as particularly deficient. The performance of the discipline of economics has not caused Blaug to abandon logical positivism and falsification. He has recently renewed his charge to his profession to live up to the standards of the true methodological orthodoxy of their discipline (Blaug, 1992).

What Blaug does not acknowledge is that certain areas of economic theory have been developed in a way that facilitates falsificationist methodology. Unambiguous falsifiable propositions have been derived from the neoclassical theories of the household and of the firm. In both theories the actions of the relevant decision-making unit are represented as solutions to a constrained extremum problem. In the case of the household, this takes the form of maximizing utility subject to a budget constraint.

For the firm, the objective is either to minimize factor outlays required to produce an arbitrary level of output or to maximize profits. The achievement of both objectives is restricted by the technological limits imposed by the production function. The distinction between exogenous and endogenous variables is unambiguous. Given that the theory presumes that households and firms are successful in achieving their desired optima, the mathematics of constrained optimization can be used to derive characteristics of relationships that describe the behaviour of either the household or the firm as it adjusts from optimum to optimum in response to changing prices, incomes, output levels or technology.

Mathematically, the formal structure of the two theories have much in common. All of the refutable hypotheses are derived from the negative or positive semi-definiteness of the matrix of comparative statics adjustments to changes in exogenous variables, in the symmetry of that comparative statics matrix and the homogeneity properties of household demand functions and the firm's profit, cost, factor demand and output supply functions. These form the basis for the empirical tests of correspondence of the theory. Appelbaum (1978) has also identified how duality theorems also can be used to test the coherence of the theory. Logical positivism upholds the importance of coherence as a criterion for theory appraisal. Appelbaum's work illustrates that tests of coherence can serve as indirect tests of correspondence.

Two recent contributions, Cozzarin and Gilmour (forthcoming) and Fox and Kivanda (1994), have surveyed the track record of the neoclassical theory of household demand and of production, factor demand and product supply. These surveys focus on the extent to which these theories have been exposed to the tests required by falsificationist methodology. They also summarize the incidence of failure to falsify when those tests have been conducted.

Fox and Kivanda (1994) examined the production economics literature. They reviewed every paper that used econometric techniques to estimate a cost function, a profit function or a system of related factor demand, factor share or product supply functions published in a sample of nine agricultural economics journals between 1976 and 1991. The *American Journal of Agricultural Economics*, the *Journal of Agricultural Economics*, the *Australian Journal of Agricultural Economics*, the *Canadian Journal of Agricultural Economics*, the *Review of Marketing and Agricultural Economics* and the four so-called regional journals of agricultural and resource economics in the United States were included in the survey.

The results of their review confirm Blaug's assessment that economists have been reluctant to expose their theories to possible falsification. Fox and Kivanda considered four falsifiable hypotheses derived from the neoclassical theory of production (Figure 4.1). Homogeneity of degree one in prices for cost and profit functions is implied by the theory. Homogeneity of degree zero is implied for factor demand and product supply functions. The negative or positive semi-definiteness of the matrix of comparative statics effects is expressed in the monotonicty of own price effects, the appropriate curvature of the cost or profit function and in the symmetry of cross-price effects. The theory predicts that cost functions should be concave in factor prices and profit functions should be convex in factor and product prices.

Seventy papers were identified in the nine journals that met the criteria used in the survey. Of these 70 papers, 32, or more than 45 per cent, tested none of the refutable hypotheses at all. Only one paper of the population of 70 tested all of the relevant falsifiable hypotheses for the theory that it employed! A summary of the findings of the Fox and Kivanda survey is presented in Table 4.1. The results of the tests of the individual hypotheses is presented in Table 4.2. Homogeneity was tested infrequently and was rejected half of the time that it was tested. Convexity and concavity were tested in almost 45 per cent of the papers and were not falsified more than two-thirds of the time. Monotonicity was tested almost 39 per cent of the time and was rarely rejected. Symmetry was tested only 17 per cent of the time and was rejected in about one-third of the cases.

The Cozzarin and Gilmour paper surveys recent contributions to the estimation of systems of demand functions for consumer goods. They identify 66 articles that report the results of efforts to estimate systems of demand functions for consumer goods. These articles appeared in 19 journals of applied or empirical economics. Almost 90 per cent of the articles stated or derived the falsifiable hypotheses of the neoclassical theory of consumption (see Figure 4.2). A consistently Popperian methodology requires that the theory pass a test of correspondence before it is used to derive elasticity estimates or for simulations. Cozzarin and Gilmour, however, report that this protocol is rarely followed. Only two articles out of the 66 actually tested the four falsifiable hypotheses implied by the theory (Table 4.3). One of these failed to reject all four of the hypotheses and one rejected two hypotheses. Tables 4.3 and 4.4 indicate that most studies only tested one or two hypotheses and that the rate of rejection was high. Table 4.5 summarizes the results for test of individual hypotheses. Even when a study by Brenton is excluded,[6] individual hypotheses were tested only about one-third of the time. When tested, the rate of rejection was about 50 per cent.

The most disturbing finding, at least from Popperian perspective, is the widespread practice of imposing the four falsifiable hypotheses as maintained assumptions. There is no basis for this practice, according to falsificationism. Cozzarin and Gilmour speculate that this imposition of hypotheses as so-called 'theoretical restrictions' often follows the rejection of the hypothesis in an earlier and unreported test.

The falsificationist methodology has clear implications regarding the relationship between theory appraisal and theory application. Theory must pass the bar of possible falsification before it is added to the provisionally accepted body of scientific knowledge. Application of theories that have faced the possibility of refutation and survived is to be undertaken with caution. Science, according to the falsificationist position, cannot *prove* the validity of

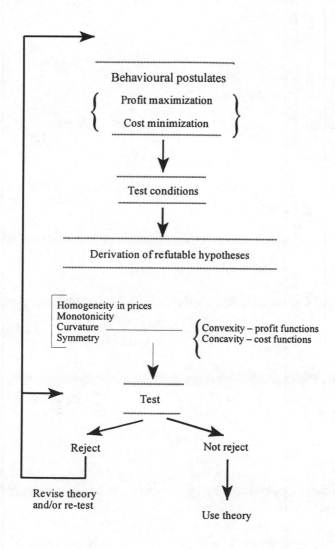

Figure 4.1 The falsifiable hypotheses of static production theory

Table 4.1 Testing neoclassical production theory (total sample, nine agricultural economics journals, 1976–1991)

Category	Number of Hypotheses Tested	Number of articles (percentages)	Results of hypothesis tests				
			Four not rejected	Three not rejected	Two not rejected	One not rejected	All rejected
No hypotheses tested	0	32 (45.7)					
Hypotheses tested	1	6 (8.6)	–	–	–	2	4
	2	23 (32.9)	–	–	18	4	0
	3	8 (11.4)	–	3	1	2	2
	4	1 (1.4)	1	0	0	0	0
Subtotal		38 (54.3)					
Total		70 (100)					

Source: Fox and Kivanda (1994), Table 1, p. 5

Table 4.2   Testing and success rates for specific hypotheses of neoclassical production theory (70 articles, 1976–1991)

Frequency	Hypothesis			
	Homogeneity	Monotonicity	Curvature	Symmetry
Tested	6	27	32	12
(%)[a]	(8.5)	(38.6)	(45.7)	(17.1)
Not rejected	3	26	22	8
(%)[b]	(50.0)	(96.3)	(68.8)	(66.7)

Notes
a.   (number of tests ÷70) × 100%.
b.   (number of failures to reject ÷ number of tests) × 100%.

any proposition, it can only have failed, so far, to falsify it. Failure to falsify is no guarantee of truthfulness. Application of theory that has not been faced with the possibility of falsification, or that has faced this test and been falsified, is not consistent with logical positivist falsificationist methodology. Nevertheless, both Cozzarin and Gilmour and Fox and Kivanda report that this practice is widespread. The rhetoric used by economists to describe the falsifiable hypotheses of the theories of the household and the firm has done much to confuse the uninitiated. It may have also befuddled its creators. Economists are fond of referring to the refutable hypotheses implied by these theories as theoretical restrictions or theoretical properties that were imposed in order to obtain efficient estimates of parameters. This practice requires an independent demonstration that the hypothesis being maintained has been tested and not falsified elsewhere and that the results of this test apply in the present context. Of course, this requirement is almost never satisfied.

ATTEMPTS TO PROTECT THE THEORY

A good falsificationist has a love–hate relationship with the theory that he or she has created. Enormous effort goes into the development of a theory and the derivation of its falsifiable hypotheses. Years of study may be required to master economic theory and the techniques used in empirical work in the discipline. Once a theory has been developed, however, its creator undergoes a 'Jekyll and Hyde' transformation. The agenda now turns to attempts to falsify this theory. This change in orientation is not easy. It should be no surprise, therefore, to find that economists have sometimes gone to great lengths to rationalize their reluctance to expose economic theories to potential falsification or that they might be tempted to discount indications of falsification when they occur. This behaviour was anticipated by Popper,

---

Axioms of Consumer Choice

1. Relexivity – each bundle is as good as itself
2. Completeness – any two bundles can be compared and ranked
3. Consistency – if 'A' is preferred over 'B', and 'B' is preferred over 'C', then 'A' is preferred over 'C'
4. Continuity – smooth indifference curves
5. Non–satiation – utility is non–decreasing in all arguments and increasing in at least one
6. Convexity – indifference curves are convex from the origin implying that the utility function is quasi–concave

Falsifiable hypotheses of demand theory

1. Adding–up – the budget constraint is satisfied
2. Monotonicity – budget shares all greater than zero
3. Homogeneity – no money illusion
4. Symmetry – cross-price effects on Hicksian demand are equal
5. Negativity – substitution matrix is negative semi–definite

---

Source: Cozzarin and Gilmour (forthcoming).

Figure 4.2 Axioms of consumer choice and propositions of demand theory

making him a shrewd social psychologist as well as a philosopher of science. He called it 'immunizing stratagems'. Not surprisingly, he was sharply critical of this type of behaviour.

Economists have employed various immunizing stratagems. A popular way of deflecting criticism of a theory is to blame a falsification on the data. The data can be deficient on several dimensions. Both the theories of the household and of the theories of the firm are developed with individual decision-making units in mind. In the theory of the firm, the optimality conditions for input use and for the level of output relate to single enterprises. In early empirical work, much of the available data were aggregated at a level higher than individual households and firms. Even with less aggregative data sets, the diversity of household consumption patterns and production activities of firms makes it necessary to aggregate across commodities and factors. For example, not all households consume creamed cheese, so demand is often expressed as demand for an aggregate category of commodities such as dairy products or even consumer non-durables. These aggregate commodity groupings do not correspond to the consumption choices that the theory has in

Table 4.3 Testing neoclassical consumption theory (total sample, 19 journals, 1980–1994)

Category	Number of hypotheses tested	Number of models	Results of Hypothesis Tests				
			Four not rejected	Three not rejected	Two not rejected	One not rejected	All rejected
No tests of propositions	0	42 12.7%					
Propositions tested	1	214 64.8%				44	170
	2	58 17.6%			24	4	30
	3	14 4.2%		7	5		2
	4	2 0.6%	1		1		
Subtotal		288 87.3%					
Total		330 100%					

Source: Cozzarin and Gilmour (forthcoming)

Table 4.4 *Testing neoclassical consumption theory (total sample, 19 journals, 1980–1994, Brenton study excluded)*

Category	Number of hypotheses tested	Number of models	Results of Hypothesis Tests				
			Four not rejected	Three not rejected	Two not rejected	One not rejected	All rejected
No tests of propositions	0	42 32.6%					
Propositions tested	1	13 10.1%				4	9
	2	58 45.0%			24	4	30
	3	14 10.9%		7	5		2
	4	2 1.6%	1		1		
Subtotal		87 67.4%					
Total		129 100%					

Source: Cozzarin and Gilmour (forthcoming).

Table 4.5 Testing and success rates for specific hypotheses of neoclassical consumption theory

Frequency	Proposition			
	Homogeneity	Monotonicity	Negativity	Symmetry
Number of hypothesis tests (%)*	37 (11)	46 (14)	252 (76)	47 (14)
Number of hypotheses not rejected (%)**	16 (43)	23 (50)	67 (27)	23 (49)
Number of hypothesis tests (excluding Brenton study) (%)#	37 (29)	46 (36)	51 (40)	47 (36)
Number of hypotheses not rejected (excluding Brenton study) (%)##	16 (43)	23 (50)	27 (53)	23 (49)

Notes
*   [(Number of Tests)/330]*100.
** [(Acceptance Rate)/Number of Tests]*100.
#   [(Number of Tests)/129]*100.
[(Acceptance Rate)/Number of Tests]*100.

Source: Cozzarin and Gilmour, (forthcoming) .

mind for the household. Similarly, not all firms use IBM computers. Some use Macintosh computers and others use manual systems to manage information. Some use electricity to heat their facilities. Others use oil and still others use natural gas. Aggregation of inputs into categories such as information management, capital assets and energy does a disservice to the types of choices that the theory sees the firm making. So the nature of economic data provides a possible explanation for the observed high rate of falsification of the theory

This explanation has severe consequences for the commonplace practice of economists, however. If the data are aggregated to the extent that they cannot provide a valid test of the theory, then they also would be unable to serve as the basis of the application of that theory. Estimates of the elasticities of demand for consumer goods, for factors of production, of output supply or measures of economies of size, scale or scope are also invalidated by problems of aggregation. Few economists seem willing to live with this level of consistency.

OBSTACLES TO AN EMPIRICIST METHODOLOGY

The most distinctive feature of an empiricist methodology is its claim that observation is the only legitimate source of scientific knowledge about the external world. This claim creates several important problems of verification. The problem of induction has already been discussed earlier in this chapter. In addition, empiricists need to resolve what is often called the Quine–Duhem thesis, the problem of theory dependency in observation, the problem of observational equivalency of competing theories and what I refer to as the problem of foundations. This last problem has to do with the origins of empiricist methodology.

Economists seem to be well aware of the Quine–Duhem thesis. This thesis states that all hypothesis tests are joint tests of the relevant theory as well as of the accuracy of data collection and measurement, the reliability of calculations and the appropriateness of the estimation procedures. This realization, however, does not validate the apparently widespread practice of discounting the testimony of the data when it is uncomfortable and accepting it when it suits our prior expectations.

Part of economists' failure to follow the precepts of falsificationism may be the product of a longstanding controversy about what parts of a theory should be tested. Most economists follow Silberberg and claim that the behavioural postulates of a neoclassical microeconomic theory are untestable, at least directly.[7] These postulates include such cherished axioms as households maximize utility, firms maximize profits and individuals maximize expected utility. Some economists such as Machina, Allais, Knetsch and Kahnemann have tested these postulates (see Machina, 1987, for an overview). Rather than treat these axioms as primitive terms, these researchers have interpreted them as predictions derived from a general notion of rationality under specific environmental conditions.

The problem of theory dependence challenges the empiricist characterization of the process of observation. The notion of theory dependence implies that even scientists do not observe in a vacuum. In particular, observation is influenced by the theory that the scientist has in mind. Theories influence the types of things that researchers try to observe. Observation is a purposive activity. It often requires a great deal of preparation and effort. The theory that the scientist has in mind influences the choice of what variables he or she attempts to observe. Observation does not take place against the objective backdrop that empiricism assumes. If observation is theory dependent, this implies that some category of knowledge precedes experience. This is antithetical to positivism.

The problem of theory dependence has figured prominently in what has been called the New Classical Macroeconomics literature, but it has arisen elsewhere in economics. Economic data are, for the most part non-experimental. They are historical. Collinearity and confounding are commonplace. It is often not possible for economists to construct decisive tests of rival theories because the data are not, in a sense, informative enough. Theories may be observationally equivalent in the sense that they have identical empirical consequences.

The problem of foundations has to do with the way in which the postulates of logical positivism were developed. Empiricist methodologies claim to set standards for the authentication of knowledge claims about the external world. Logical positivism is a set of propositions about the origins and structure of meaningful statements about the external world. All meaningful statements about the external world are subject to the requirements of logical positivism. But logical positivism itself aspires to be a meaningful statement about the external world, at least about that portion of the external world that is called science. Logical positivism requires that only synthetic statements can be meaningful and it insists that the only basis for validation of synthetic statements is observation. Unfortunately, this requirement is not consistent with itself. If this statement is a synthetic statement, its validation did not originate in observation or experience. If it is an analytic statement, it is, by definition, not meaningful. The doctrines of logical positivism were not authenticated in a manner that satisfies its own methodological standard. Logical positivism is hoist with its own petard!

CRITICS OF LOGICAL POSITIVISM AND FALSIFICATIONISM

The marriage of logical positivism and Popperian falsificationism may be the dominant methodological position in economics, but its acceptance is not universal. Since these empiricist methodological doctrines constitute the closest thing to a mainstream view in economics, it should not be surprising that several critical attacks have been mounted. Hollis and Nell (1975, pp. 3–10) and McCloskey (1985, pp. 5–11) have compiled lists of the ten commandments of empiricism or logical positivism in economic methodology.

These lists are really descriptions of the most popular methodological propositions in contemporary economics, and as such contain ideas that are not always purely positivist. For example, several aspects of instrumentalism, to be discussed in the next chapter, are included. Nevertheless, much of the modernism that McCloskey rejects and of the empiricism Hollis and Nell repudiate are based on logical positivism and falsificationism.

Critics have attacked the empiricist methodological school on three fronts. Some writers have argued that economists who subscribe to logical positivism have been caught unaware in a philosophical time capsule. They continue to uphold methodological views that have been long rejected by philosophers of science. This is the message in the title of Bruce Caldwell's (1982) *Beyond Positivism: Economic Methodology in the Twentieth Century*. One thread in this line of criticism is that economists have misunderstood Popper in two ways. First, the Popper of *Conjectures and Refutations* of 1963 holds a different view from the Popper of *The Logic of Scientific Discovery* of 1935. In addition, it has been suggested that Popper's views on the methodology of the social sciences have not been well integrated into the thinking of economic methodologists.[8]

The Popper of 1963 does not abandon falsificationism, but he does advance a sort of 'kinder and gentler' version of the doctrine. He outlines a position that he calls 'Critical Rationalism' (see Table 4.6 for a synopsis of Popper's critical rationalism). Like Hollis and Nell and McCloskey, Popper follows the pattern of Moses and David Letterman by expressing the main elements of critical rationalism in ten theses (1963/1989, pp. 27–9).[9] Critical rationalism rejects the positivist view that observation is the only source of knowledge. Popper rejects the idea of ultimate sources of knowledge. The origin of a proposition is not important. What matters is its truthfulness. We have not been able to agree on a criterion for truth, but we do have indications of error. Lack of clarity is one possible indicator. Lack of clarity does not necessarily indicate error, but it should make us suspicious. Similarly, inconsistency, when discovered, is a 'dim red light'. I believe that Popper is appealing to the asymmetry between demonstration of truth and refutation discussed earlier. Verification is an impossible standard. It requires a general or universal proof. Falsification needs only a single counter-example.

The Popper of 1963 sees the scientific enterprise as a process of conjecture and refutation. Conjecture is the beginning of the process. Even pre-science, what Popper calls myths, can be the starting point. What follows is a process of criticism, using both observation and reason, during which we try to root out errors embodied in initial conjectures. This is a method of trial and error. Conjectures are often bold leaps, made with as little as a single observation. The essential ingredient in a scientific approach to a subject is a deep and abiding commitment to the process of criticism. Critical rationalism is a prescription for the activities of the community of scientists in a particular field. It says as much about the quality and the nature of their disciplinary

Table 4.6 Popper's ten theses of critical rationalism

1. There are no ultimate sources of knowledge. Every source is open to criticism.
2. The important question is not the source of a statement, but whether the statement is true.
3. Examination of the truthfulness of a statement may proceed on multiple lines, including both coherence and correspondence.
4. The most important source of knowledge is tradition.
5. Without tradition, for example, without the tradition describing the appropriate way to give and receive criticism, knowledge is not possible. But even tradition is open to criticism.
6. Knowledge can not start from nothing. Advances in knowledge, in the main, consist of modifications to existing knowledge.
7. We do not possess a criterion for truth, but we do have criteria that enable us to recognize error. Clarity distinctness and coherence are not criteria of truth, but they may indicate error.
8. Neither observation nor reason is an authority. Both of these faculties assist in criticism.
9. Exactness is not valuable in and of itself. There is no point in being more precise than the circumstances require. Linguistic precision is a phantom.
10. The more that we know about the world, the greater the knowledge of our ignorance.

Source: Based on Popper (1963/1989, pp. 27–9).

interaction as it does about the content of their deliberations. Critical rationalism is an attitude that all knowledge claims are provisional and that clarity in proposition and rigour in criticism are the goal of interaction in the scientific community.

It is possible that economists have done a disservice to Popper in failing to recognize the distinctions between logical positivism and his ideas about conjectures and refutations and criticism. Popper's rejection of the positivists' claim that the exclusive origin of meaningful statements about the external world is observation is fundamental. In practice, as I will argue at greater length in Chapter 6, economists have been loath to give up reason, intuition and introspection as sources of knowledge about the external world of human social interaction.

Hausman (1988), Caldwell (1982) and Hoppe (1988) have summarized the case against logical positivism and falsification. Neither logical positivism nor Popperian falsificationism has solved the problem of induction. The logic of an inductive proof of a law-like universal statement based on particular observations still eludes us. Falsificationism merely shifts the problem of induction to the level of the set of propositions that have not been falsified so far. Is a hypothesis that has withstood two harsh attempts to falsify more or less valid than one that has withstood only one test? Our intuition wants to say yes, but neither logical positivism nor falsificationism furnishes arguments to support that intuition.

THE METHODOLOGY OF SCIENTIFIC RESEARCH PROGRAMMES

Lakatos (1978) has called for a broader interpretation of the falsificationist agenda. According to this broader interpretation it is research programmes and not individual hypotheses that should be the object of falsification.[10] A research programme consists of three elements: the hard core, the protective belt and a positive heuristic. The hard core is the collection of basic axioms or hypotheses that constitute the irrefutable central ideas of a field of study. The hard core effectively defines what is distinctive about a research programme. To reject or abandon the hard core is to abandon the research programme itself. The protective belt consists of the refutable hypotheses derived from the axioms of the hard core. The positive heuristic describes how the research programme is to be undertaken. This includes a consensus view on research strategies and standards for the authentication of claims of contributions to knowledge. It is not as central to the identity of the programme as is the hard core and in fact the positive heuristic may evolve as the programme proceeds.

In the methodology of scientific research programmes, the crucial determination to be made is whether a particular research programme is progressive or degenerating. A progressive research programme has better or more content than its rivals and is more fruitful in anticipating novel events. A degenerating research programme fails to exhibit these attributes and its practitioners devote considerable effort to protecting the programme from its critics. The practical significance of the methodology of scientific research programmes is a call for tolerance. Scientists in a discipline should be lenient in their appraisals of new research programmes, because new research programmes need time to achieve progressiveness. In addition, scientists should be tolerant of old research programmes that have fallen into degeneration, because they might become progressive in the future. Some sceptics have described this as an 'anything goes' methodology. I find it hard to be critical of a call for tolerance in general, but the criteria for theory appraisal articulated in the methodology of scientific research programmes seem to provide few objective standards for theory appraisal in economics.

CONCLUSION

We have arrived at an unhappy destination. If we accept the idea that the mainstream view of scientific methodology held by economists is a hybrid of logical positivism and the falsificationism of Sir Karl Popper, it is difficult to resist the conclusion that this fusion has produced sterile offspring. Economists have shown a deep and abiding reluctance to follow a strict falsificationist methodology.[11] Whether it is impossible or merely difficult to follow this methodology in economics is still an open question.

QUESTIONS FOR DISCUSSION

1. What is a falsifiable hypothesis?
2. Evaluate the criticisms of logical positivism that have been raised by economic methodologists.
3 If economists adopted Popper's ten theses of critical rationalism, how do you think economics would change?

NOTES

1. Milton Friedman's influential essay of 1953, to be discussed in the next chapter, used the term positivism to denote a methodological doctrine that is now recognized as instrumentalism. Unfortunately, the substantial literature spawned by Friedman's essay has generally failed to acknowledge his idiosyncratic use of the term positivism and a great deal of confusion has resulted.
2. *A priorism* is discussed in Chapter 6.
3. Issue No.1 of Volume 1, published in January 1933.
4. Ironically, Mises also draws on Kant's distinction between analytic and synthetic statements. He reaches very different conclusions regarding economic methodology, however (see Chapter 6).
5. See his *The Structure of Economic Analysis: A Mathematical Analysis* (1978), Chapter 1, Section 1.3. Silberberg does not claim to be a methodologist, but few economists do. Nevertheless, most textbook writers seem to be compelled to articulate their interpretation of methodological orthodoxy in the introductory chapters of their books. Silberberg is no exception.
6. The Brenton study accounted for some 201 model specifications and tests.
7. See Boland (1981).
8. See Caldwell (1991), and de Marchi (ed.) (1992).
9. We are fortunate that the ten item list of Moses and Letterman has been more popular than the approach of Martin Luther, who required 97 theses to state his point of view.
10. See Latsis (ed.) (1976) for a selection of essays that explore the application of Lakatos's views in economics.

11. There is some anecdotal evidence that the editorial policies of journals are partially responsible for this situation. Authors are reluctant to report falsifications because they perceive that this increases the risk of a manuscript being rejected.

5. Economics As Prediction

INTRODUCTION

Most lists of the axioms of methodological orthodoxy in economics combine ideas from logical positivism and Popperian falsificationism with instrumentalism. Milton Friedman's (1953) influential essay 'The Methodology of Positive Economics' is one of the strongest statements of the instrumentalist position in the economics literature. It is regrettable that Friedman used the term 'Positive economics' to describe his views. This notion of positivism is different from the views of the logical positivists discussed in the last chapter. Only recently has the relationship between Friedman's 'positive economics' and the well–established methodological doctrine of instrumentalism been clarified. Instrumentalism has been the traditional chief rival of scientific realism (see Chapter 7) among philosophies of science. Until recently, however, the contest in economics has been one-sided.

INSTRUMENTALISM AND THE FOUR KEY METHODOLOGICAL QUESTIONS

What is the Purpose of Economic Analysis?

As the name suggests, instrumentalism treats theories as instruments. As instruments, theories should be assessed on the basis of their usefulness. In economics, this usefulness criterion has been interpreted, at least since Friedman, as success in prediction. Instrumentalists maintain that truthfulness, particularly truthfulness in representation, is not a relevant criterion for theory appraisal. To an instrumentalist, therefore, the purpose of economic theory is to produce accurate and reliable predictions. Theories do not possess any descriptive meaning about the true nature of phenomena. Theory may also serve as a language or logical lexicon to help economists arrange their thoughts and to communicate with one another.

To an instrumentalist, the purpose of theory leads naturally to criteria for theory appraisal. The proof of the pudding is in the predicting. Instrumentalists have a singular test of correspondence. The point of contact between theory and phenomena is the prediction and only the prediction. As we will see later in this chapter, Friedman is particularly unequivocal on this point. On other basic methodological questions, instrumentalists dismiss the problem of induction as irrelevant. What does it matter that an empirical record of confirmation or failure to falsify cannot prove the truthfulness of a proposition if truthfulness is not a meaningful criterion for theory appraisal? Instrumentalists have also been critical of any methodological doctrine that invokes a notion of essentialism. They have viewed attempts to explain the essence or the true meaning that undergirds the observable as misguided metaphysics.

On the meanings of prediction in economics

The word prediction is used to describe several types of statements in economics. For example, the statement 'On 1 August, 199X, the prime rate charged by Canadian Chartered banks will be 8.2 per cent' is one type of prediction. It is quantitative and dated. It is not a conditional statement of the form 'If X occurs then Y will occur'. I prefer to call this type of prediction a forecast. Non–economists often see the purpose of economics as the production of forecasts, and a large number of what we might call business economists are involved in just this type of activity. Other economic predictions are conditional. For example, the statement 'If the tariff rate on imported wool cloth is eliminated then the profits of domestic manufacturers of wool cloth will fall' is a conditional prediction. Rosenberg (1992) argues that all scientific predictions are of this type. If the conditions do not hold, then all bets are off. Economic predictions of this type invoke the so-called *ceteris paribus* condition. That is, in addition to the requirement that the tariff on wool textiles be eliminated, the prediction regarding the profits of domestic manufacturers also requires that no other factors vary. For example, if domestic manufacturers introduce a new product line or a new process technology then profits could actually increase after the elimination of the import tariff. Or a bilateral elimination of tariffs between two trading partners may create improved opportunities for exports for domestic firms. An economic conditional prediction presumes that variables like these do not vary if the predicted outcome is to occur. These predictions can be described as counter–factual when they are retroactive. For example, economists might predict how the evolution of an economy might have been different if a policy decision had been made differently in the past. In this case, economists are predicting what the world would have been like. Instead of an 'as if' statement, this is an 'if only' statement.

According to Rosenberg (1992), improved accuracy of conditional predictions requires more accurate determination of whether the initial conditions hold and increased precision in the characterization of the mechanisms that link these conditions and the predicted phenomena. Instrumentalists are suspicious of the second route to theory improvement. It sounds too much like an invocation of truthfulness as a criterion for theory appraisal. But Rosenberg argues that the first route is not feasible. At a fundamental level, the initial conditions cannot be independently tested in economics. Observation of apparent intransitivity of preferences could occur because people are actually acting irrationally, or it could be that their preferences have changed. Without an independent means of objectively measuring changes in preferences, instrumentalist economists cannot distinguish between these two situations. In Rosenberg's (1992, p. 128) view, 'The theory of rational choice is condemned to predictive sterility' and later (p. 239), 'the explanatory variables of economic theory ... are not linked to physical mechanisms in a way that will enable us to discover where and how they go wrong'. Preferences, beliefs and expectations, the antecedents of the human actions that instrumentalist economists seek to predict, are not objectively measurable. As a result, when predictions go wrong, we cannot ever really know why. Rosenberg's conclusions show a remarkable similarity to the methodological writings of Mises (see Chapter 6), but they are reached by a very different route.

George Stigler and Gary Becker (1977) offer an escape from this dilemma, by assuming it away. Their title, in translation, is 'Don't quarrel over tastes'. In the context of economic theory, they maintain that this should be interpreted to mean 'that tastes neither change capriciously nor differ importantly between people. On this interpretation one does not argue over tastes for the same reason that one does not argue over the Rocky Mountains – both are there, will be next year, too, and are the same to all men' (p. 76). So differences in behaviour among individuals are the consequence of differences in circumstances such as incomes and prices and not the result of differences in preferences. This perspective is preferred, in their assessment, on the basis of 'comparative analytical productivities'. They then proceed to study examples of human behaviour: addiction, habitual behaviour, advertising and fashions. These phenomena have traditionally been considered a challenge to the notion of identical and stable preferences. Stigler and Becker, using the household production model, show that a covering law model of explanation can be used for each of these examples. In each case, behavioural differences are explained exclusively in terms of differences in prices and incomes. What Stigler and Becker do not acknowledge is that there is more import to their task than the exploration of analytical productivity. Their thesis is necessary to explicate Friedman's instrumentalist methodology from the quagmire of subjectivism described by Rosenberg and Hausman (1992). Predictive success could not be improved in a world with unobservable, subjective diverse and unstable preferences. It is at least possible in a Stigler – Becker world, because the *ceteris paribus* conditions are all objectively observable.

A third class of predictions has been described as 'Pattern Predictions'. This term was introduced by Hayek. Discussion of this type of prediction is deferred until Chapter 6. It really is a fundamentally different notion that the instrumentalist idea of prediction. It is the type of prediction sought in the understanding tradition. Instrumentalism falls more into the explanation view, but as I will argue later, it aspires to a very limited type of explanation.

Economists also make possibility predictions. These are of the form 'Observed situation X, such as cyclical fluctuations in output and employment, can occur as the consequence of interaction of rational individual decision makers'. The rational expectations literature makes these types of predictions. Here, models of rational optimizing agents that interact in markets that are always and everywhere in equilibrium are shown to exhibit cycle-like behaviour under particular circumstances. The purpose of this type of possibility prediction is to show that appeals to irrationality or disequilibrium are not necessary to the construction of coherent explanations of economic fluctuations.

Economists also make what we might call 'impossibility predictions'. These are predictions of the 'There is no such thing as a free lunch' variety. Arrow's (1951) impossibility theorem is such a prediction. A number of predictions derived from the notion of scarcity, as well as statements such as 'increasing returns to scale cannot be the general situation in firms' also fit in this category.

Rosenberg, Hausman and Leontief share the view that predictive success is a reasonable criterion for the appraisal of economic theory, but they also seem to accept that the track record of economics on this score is not impressive. Evaluation of the degree of predictive success of economics is not a trivial task. Economics is a diverse enterprise and internal controversies abound. Evaluation of the individual predictive success record of each of the distinctive schools of thought within economics would be daunting.

More fundamentally, Friedman and others who have invoked this standard for theory appraisal have not thoroughly explored the meanings of the idea of prediction. There are several notions of 'prediction'. Which one should be used in the assessment of economic theory?

I think that Friedman was primarily concerned with what I have called conditional predictions. Assessment of conditional predictions is complex. Not only do we have to determine if X happened, we also need to know if Y occurred. Most of the predictions of economic theory are conditional. The prediction of the neoclassical theory of production that the level of production will not fall if the price of the firm's output rises, is conditional on the familiar *ceteris paribus* requirements. If the price of the firm's inputs increases at the same time as the increase in output price, all bets are off. Testing this prediction of theory requires a determination that the effects of variables that act jointly on the variable of interest be isolated. As Rosenberg (1992) and Hausman (1992) have demonstrated, in economics this is ultimately impossible to do. All economic predictions are derived from some notion of rationality. Human action is interpreted as an attempt to improve the circumstances of an actor, given that actors' preferences and perceptions of opportunities for action. But preferences and perceptions lie outside the theory. They are treated as exogenous. Economic theory does not contain a theory of preference determination or change. Some naive theories of perception have been proposed, but without some means of independent and objective characterization of preferences, theories of perceptions, or 'expectations' cannot be validated. Any action can be reconciled with the notion of rationality because preferences can take on a number of forms and may change. Stigler and Becker's (1977) claim that economic theory requires that individuals be considered to have identical and immutable preferences is in one sense correct. If this condition is not met, then any observed human action is consistent with the economist's notion of rationality.

Conditional predictions implicitly invoke causality. If the condition X is necessary for event Y to occur, then X is a causal factor in the occurrence of Y. There may be multiple causal factors, and hence many conditions that need to be established in the prediction of event Y.

Predictions can also be categorized as qualitative or quantitative. Qualitative predictions state a direction of change for a variable. For example *X will rise.* Quantitative predictions say something about the magnitude of that change. A statement of the form *X will increase by 15 per cent* is an example of a quantitative prediction.

What is the Source of Economic Knowledge?

Instrumentalists, at least in economics, have been more inclusive regarding the legitimate sources of knowledge than the logical positivists. Perhaps the affirmation of usefulness as a criterion for theory appraisal has caused them to accept human introspection as a useful source of knowledge. In any case, Friedman acknowledges the peculiar status of the social science researcher as an insider in the system being studied. Instrumentalists do not generally go so far as to reject the unity of science position of the logical positivists, however.

There is an implicit hierarchy of sources of knowledge regarding theory validation in economic instrumentalism. Remember that, to an economic instrumentalist, the proof of the pudding is in the predicting. Successful prediction is evaluated in terms of regularities in relationships among observables. Presumptions about the constancy of unobservables, such as the subjective preferences of individuals, are used to establish the primacy of observables in the evaluation of theories. So while introspection may be useful in the generation of hypotheses, it gives way to observation in the validation of theories based on those hypotheses.

What is the Scope of Economic Analysis?

Instrumentalism, at least as it has been practised by Friedman and his University of Chicago colleagues like Gary Becker and George Stigler, has been eager to extend the scope of economic inquiry into more and more areas of human behaviour and interaction. The economics of information, crime and punishment, marriage, fertility and divorce are just some of the frontiers that have been colonized. Like the logical positivists, instrumentalists have not shown much interest in delimiting the scope of economics. The one requirement, and this is implicit in the essay by Becker and Stigler, is that economic analysis should confine itself to the realm of objective observation in the appraisal of theories.

What is the Appropriate Structure of Economic Theory?

The structure of economic theory, according to instrumentalism, is illustrated in Figures 5.1 and 5.2. Figure 5.1 addresses a common misunderstanding of Friedman's position on the unrealisticness of assumptions. It is sometimes suggested that Friedman advocated unrealisticness in assumptions for its own sake. This is incorrect. Friedman stated that 'Significant Theories', in economics or any other field, always had unrealistic assumptions. This does not mean that unrealistic assumptions are sufficient for significance, just that they are necessary.

Figure 5.2 bears a superficial resemblance to the logical positivist structure attributed to Eugene Silberberg in the previous chapter. Since both logical positivism and instrumentalism are empiricist methodologies, this resemblance might be expected. There is an important distinction between the two views, however. The behavioural postulates that form the foundation for theory in Silberberg's model are not subject to direct testing because they are unobservable. The indirect testing protocol, however, maintains the importance of testing as an assessment of truthfulness of a theory. There is no question that truthfulness is a relevant criterion. The only question is where is truthfulness to be assessed? Instrumentalists deny the relevance of truthfulness in theory appraisal. The axioms of theory, according to an instrumentalist, are not being tested for truthfulness, even indirectly.

THE METHODOLOGY OF POSITIVE ECONOMICS

Friedman's 1953 essay has been one of the most influential and controversial contributions to the literature of economics methodology in the twentieth century. It spawned its own critical literature, even though Friedman has never responded in writing to any of his critics. The controversy surrounding the logical status of the behavioural postulates employed in the neoclassical theory of the firm, as that theory was being formalized in the two decades preceding Friedman's essay, served as the backdrop or perhaps even the motivation for his instrumentalism. Questions such as 'Do firms really maximize profits?' or 'Do businessmen really set marginal cost equal to marginal revenue?' had

Theories with Unrealistic Assumptions

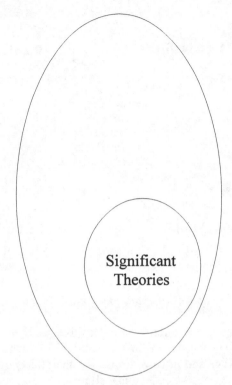

Figure 5.1   Friedman's position on the realism of assumptions and the significance of a theory

divided the profession. To an instrumentalist, viewing theory as a means to an end or as an instrument, and defining that end as reliable prediction, this debate was a tempest in a teapot. What did it matter if the behavioural postulates invoked in a theory corresponded to the actual motivations or actions of businesses if the theory predicted well?

Friedman begins his essay by invoking John Neville Keynes's distinction between a positive and a normative science. According to this distinction, a positive science consists of a systematic area of knowledge about phenomena as they exist. A normative science consists of a system of principles describing the arrangement of phenomena that ought to be. An 'art', on the other hand, is a set of guidelines or rules of thumb to assist in achieving particular ends using given means. The goal of Friedman's essay is to articulate criteria for the appraisal of economic theory in the positive mode. The motivation for this exercise is the hypothesis that virtually all of the controversies among economists on important policy issues arises from differences on factual questions and not normative ones.   Examples of

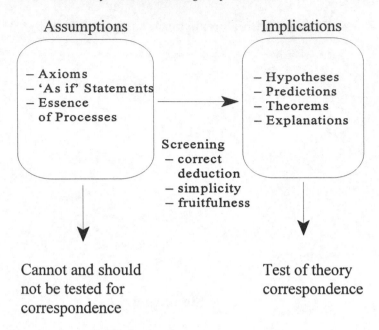

Figure 5.2   Theory appraisal under Friedman's instrumentalism

controversies animated by differences on positive questions include the effects of minimum wage legislation on the standard of living of the poor, the desirability of wage and price controls, and the effects of tariffs and other interferences with trade on economic welfare.

The purpose of this positive economic science is 'the development of a "theory" or "hypothesis" that yields valid and meaningful (i.e. not truistic) predictions about phenomena not yet observed' (1953, p. 7). The point of correspondence between theory and phenomena is prediction. The relevant standard is relative. It is the predictive success of a hypothesis relative to its most successful rival that matters, not success at prediction relative to some absolute standard. This relativity appears in another context as well. Near the end of the essay, Friedman states 'Everything depends on the problem; there is no inconsistency in regarding the same firm as if it were a perfect competitor for one problem, and a monopolist for another' (1953, p. 36).

The structure of theory consists of two elements; a language or filing system of logical categories and definitions and a body of substantive hypotheses. These hypotheses are substantive in the sense that they are intended to be statements about the way that phenomena are. In fact, Friedman describes these substantive hypotheses as 'designed to abstract essential features of complex reality' which transgresses the instrumentalists' aversion to essentialism. Formal logic is sufficient for the validation of theory as a language. This is appraisal of coherence, and is concerned with completeness and consistency. However, factual evidence alone is relevant in the appraisal of theory as a body of substantive hypotheses. And the only proper use of factual evidence in assessing the validity of a hypothesis or a theory is the correspondence of its predictions with experience. Failure to falsify is invoked as the relevant criterion in assessing this correspondence, although neither Popper nor his economist apologist Hutchison are mentioned.

Failure to falsify may still not be enough to pare down the number of alternative theories or hypotheses because of the problem of observational equivalence, that is 'Observed facts are necessarily finite in number; possible hypotheses, infinite. If there is one hypothesis that is consistent with the available evidence, there are always an infinite number that are' (1953, p. 8), so some additional criteria for theory appraisal are needed to narrow the field. Friedman suggests fruitfulness, that is, usefulness in prediction in other settings, and simplicity, defined as requiring a limited amount of information to make a prediction, as additional criteria.

By the top of the thirteenth page of the essay, Friedman has completely characterized his positive heuristic for theory appraisal. He then proceeds, not to outline the basis for this methodological position, but to attack what he viewed as a serious and pervasive error in methodological discussions of the time. He affirms that various obstacles make the empirical assessment of economic theories difficult, but that the controversy regarding the correspondence of the assumptions of a theory and phenomena, the so-called realism of assumptions, had led professional efforts in theory appraisal seriously astray. The remaining thirty pages of the essay are devoted to a discussion of the role and significance of assumptions in economic theory. As I will argue below, it is this discussion and not Friedman's positive heuristic for theory appraisal itself that has had the greatest effect on economists.

Friedman's position on assumptions is ambidextrous. On the one hand, he maintains that assumptions are not really independent statements at all, but merely components of hypotheses. On the other hand, he claims that 'Truly important and significant hypotheses will be found to have "assumptions" that are wildly inaccurate, descriptive representations of reality' (p. 14) which seems to imply that a test of unrealisticness can be applied to an assumption independent of its context as part of a hypothesis. Figure 5.1, based on Friedman's discussion, summarizes his views on the relationship between unrealisticness of assumptions and importance of the associated theory. Unrealistic assumptions are necessary but not sufficient for importance. Importance derives from predictive success, fruitfulness and simplicity and, according to Friedman, only theories with descriptively non-corresponding assumptions can ever satisfy these criteria. The class of theories with unrealistic assumptions is presumably enormous, so the scarcity of time and other research resources suggests that the criteria for significance alone be invoked.

Assumptions are nevertheless important in the structure of theories. Assumptions are often a concise way of stating a theory, provide an opportunity to test a theory indirectly, and can indicate the range of conditions over which the theory applies. The economy or conciseness in expression derives from two sources. Assumptions may be used as a summary of conditions that must be satisfied in order for the hypothesis to follow. In this capacity, assumptions take on a fable-like quality. Drawing on the botanical example of leaves on a tree, Friedman sees the assumption that leaves seek to maximize their exposure to sunlight as equivalent but more compact than a detailed enumeration of the necessary conditions for leaves to follow the trajectory of the sun. In elaborating on this role for assumptions, Friedman distinguishes between assumptions and 'crucial' assumptions. This distinction has essentialist overtones, and is a deviation from a purely instrumentalist methodology.

Friedman's discussion of the use of assumptions as an indirect test of a theory is one of the most difficult but most important sections of the essay. This is the first place in the essay that the word assumption is not used in quotation marks. He begins by claiming that the distinction between assumptions and implications, and by implications he presumably means hypotheses or predictions, is often difficult to draw. He also uses the word axiom as a synonym for assumption and theorem as a synonym for implication in this section of the essay. There are two senses in which this traditional distinction is difficult. First, through the use of an example, Friedman demonstrates that the implications of a positive economic analysis can become the axioms or starting point for a normative analysis. Unfortunately, he does not seem to be aware that his example embraces these two types of analysis. As a result it is not clear what implications the reader should draw. The second factor that blurs the distinction between assumptions and implications is the problem of observational equivalence mentioned earlier in the essay. There may be more than one set of assumptions that imply the same set of predictions. Presumably, however, this indeterminacy is addressed by the criteria of simplicity and fruitfulness.

The second type of indirect test of a theory through its assumptions involves the recognition of parallels in other theories. If a theory invokes an assumption that is also employed in another theory and that theory has a track record of successful prediction, then the hypothesis 'gains indirect plausibility'. Although Friedman (p. 23) acknowledges that assumptions can also delimit the scope of application of a theory, he does not elaborate on this function.

In the penultimate section of the essay, Friedman returns to the position that the assumptions of a theory cannot be realistic in the sense of being descriptively accurate and complete and that attempts to achieve realism in this sense would render a theory useless. His defence of this position is ultimately essentialist. In his words 'The ideal types are not intended to be descriptive;

they are designed to isolate the features that are crucial for a particular problem' (p. 36).

According to Friedman, the purpose of economic theory is to produce reliable predictions. Consequently, theories should be evaluated on the basis of their predictive record relative to other theories. The difficulty of conducting experiments in economics creates obstacles for the validation of economic hypotheses but these problems are operational and not fundamental. Economics does not, therefore, require a distinct methodology from other sciences. The problem of the observational equivalence of theories, itself a consequence of the difficulty of experimentation, is resolved through the additional criteria of simplicity and fruitfulness. The assumptions of a theory are not intended to be accurate and complete descriptions of phenomena. In fact attempts to construct theories on a foundation of assumptions that have been independently empirically validated are at best pointless and at worst harmful.

DISCUSSION

The most remarkable thing about 'The Methodology of Positive Economics' is what the essay does not contain. Friedman provides no arguments and no economic evidence to support his methodological position. The examples that he uses in the middle of the essay to illustrate the role of assumptions in theory are not from economics. There are no references to the work of other methodologists or philosophers of science. Even the obvious influence of Popper's notion of falsification is not acknowledged. There is no inventory of economic hypotheses that have successfully passed the bar of reliable prediction. Not a single example of a successful economic hypothesis is given. The neoclassical price theory, absent the apparatus of Robinson and Chamberlin, is cited with approval, but the basis for this favourable comment is unclear.

The influence of logical positivism on Friedman's instrumentalism is evident from several methodological statements in the second section of the essay. He affirms a unity of science doctrine, arguing that the lack of experimental procedures in economic research creates problems for testing predictions which are different in degree but not in kind from those faced in the natural sciences. Friedman claims that 'No experiment can be completely controlled, in the sense that some disturbing influences are relatively constant in the course of it' (p. 10).

Evidence cast up by experience is 'abundant and frequently as conclusive as that from contrived experiments' (p. 10) so that while progress in the validation of theory may be slower or more difficult in economics, it follows essentially the same protocol as the experimental sciences. Friedman also invokes Popper's falsification principal, at least in a weakened version.

'Factual evidence can never "prove" a hypothesis; it can only fail to disprove it' (p. 9) is clearly a Popperian view, but to Friedman, the relevant standard of comparison is the predictive success of the best alternative hypothesis. This is a weakened form of Popperian theory appraisal in that a prediction which had been falsified could be retained if it had been refuted less often than its strongest rival.

Friedman also acknowledges the problem of observational equivalence. He suggests (p. 9) that if one hypothesis is consistent with the available data then there is always an infinite number of hypotheses that are consistent. Choice among equally empirically successful hypotheses is to be based on the 'arbitrary ... criteria [of] "simplicity" and "fruitfulness"'. Although these criteria defy rigorous definition, they undergird the controversial position that Friedman takes on the realism of assumptions later in the essay.

In some respects Friedman is not a pure instrumentalist at all. In his discussion of assumptions, he frequently adopts an essentialist position. He sees an important and useful economic theory as one that abstracts from irrelevant details and captures the key elements or crucial aspects of a situation.

Scientific realists reject instrumentalism because it makes the progress of science a miracle. How can a theory predict reliably if it is not true? How can something that is not true be useful? Would it not be more useful if it were more true? They also maintain that instrumentalists have misunderstood the problem of apprehension of truth. Instrumentalists have sometimes argued that the determination of truthfulness is beyond the capabilities of mere mortals, even mere mortal scientists. Scientific realists counter by saying that this does not contradict the view that the goal of theory is apprehension of truth. Even if we are unable to demonstrate that a particular theory is true or false, that does not change the fact that the theory actually is true or false. The agenda of methodology is the improvement of our ability to make that determination.

THE LEGACY OF FRIEDMAN'S METHODOLOGY

Economists have largely ignored part of Friedman's message but generally embraced another part. Predictive success has not been adopted as the definitive test in theory appraisal. On the other hand, non-referential assumptions are commonplace in economic models. Friedman's essay, along with a widely-held view that economists cannot predict the future, usually expressed as some version of the efficient markets hypothesis, have effectively slipped the empirical moorings of economics at both ends. On the one hand, Friedman's view that verification of the correspondence of assumptions is both impossible and undesirable has liberated theory from appraisal at that point. It is now commonplace for economists to stand and declare, both in the classroom and in professional meetings, that they are about to invoke wildly inaccurate assumptions and nobody objects. With regard to testing the predictive record, it is also commonplace to argue that if markets are efficient, that is, that they have incorporated all of the relevant information available, including the predictions of economic theory, then economists' predictions are of no use, liberating theory from appraisal at that end.[1]

In the end, I believe that the legacy of his essay contradicts Friedman's hope that it would prompt economists to abandon the, to him, fruitless methodological controversies of his time and to pursue the development of more predictively successful economic theory.

QUESTIONS FOR DISCUSSION

1. What does Milton Friedman mean by 'prediction'?
2. Make a list of the different ways that 'assumptions' are used in economics.
3. What are some examples of economic theories that meet Friedman's methodological criteria?

NOTE

1. Richard Levins's 'On Farmers Who Solve Equations' is a satirical repudiation of this legacy.

6. Economics as Deduction

The economist starts with a knowledge of ultimate causes. He is already, at the outset of his enterprise, in the position which the physicist only attains after ages of laborious research .... He is already in possession of those ultimate principles governing the phenomena which form the object of his study .... Since we possess direct knowledge ... of causes in our consciousness of what passes in our minds.

(J.E. Cairnes, *Character and Logical Method of Political Economy,* pp. 83–90)

We can observe natural phenomena only from outside, but ourselves from within which finds for us in economic experience all the most important facts of economy

(F. Wieser, *Social Economics*, 1927/1967, p. 17)

The general aim of all science is to cover the greatest number of experimental facts by logical deduction from the smallest number of hypotheses or axioms.

(Albert Einstein, *Life*, 9 January, 1950)

INTRODUCTION

This chapter outlines the main features of an old but not currently fashionable methodological position known as *a priorism. A priorism* was an extremely influential doctrine in economics up to the mid-1930s. Nassau Senior (1836/1965), John Neville Keynes (1963) and J.E. Cairnes (1888/1965) were all advocates of *a priorism*. According to Bill Gerrard (1990), this methodological doctrine is the predominant view in economics. My view is that there are different types of *a priorism* employed by economists. The different strains of this doctrine have little in common. The thesis of this chapter is that *a priorism*, at least certain versions of it, while vilified in high places, has never been definitively refuted by its critics and continues to be an influential force in the way that economists go about their work. Because this influence is typically implicit, it often neglects to adhere to the entire protocol of *a priorism* and results in a hybridized and ultimately flawed expression of this point of view. Several twentieth century *a priorists* will be discussed in this chapter. The first is Lionel Robbins, whose influential *Essay on the Nature and Significance of Economic Science* has furnished the most frequently used definition of economics in the last half century. This chapter will also examine the methodological writings of Ludwig von Mises, Murray Rothbard, Martin Hollis and Edward Nell.

The most striking feature of *a priorism*, at least when viewed through empiricist lenses, is the idea that economic theory is predominantly a logical structure erected on a short-list of self-evident propositions or axioms. *A priorists* tend to make observation a secondary faculty to reason in the development and validation of theory. *A priorists* do not ignore the role of observation in theory validation, but they do expect it to serve a more limited function than, say, the logical positivists did.

A central theme in *a priorism* is that the social sciences are somehow fundamentally different from the natural sciences. This difference is illustrated in Figure 6.1. In the case of the natural sciences, the investigator is always in a position of observing phenomena from the outside. In the social sciences, the disciplines that study human action and human social interaction, the investigator exists as a part of the phenomena. The chemist has never been a carbon atom, but the economist is a person. This situation creates a problem and an opportunity for the social scientist. The problem is one of complexity and objectivity. The opportunity is to go beyond the limits of knowledge accessible to natural scientists. The investigator of social phenomena has access to knowledge about the purpose and meaning of the actions of his subjects. This knowledge is general, in that it is rarely possible to discern and articulate the particular purpose and meaning of specific actions, but actions are understood to have a common foundation – in Mises' words, actions are attempts to substitute more desired states of affairs for less desired ones. This knowledge is obtained *a priori*, meaning literally prior to experience, but the essential idea is that this self-knowledge is an intrinsic part of human cognition. This *a priori* knowledge occupies a central role in both the structure and the appraisal of theories. With regard to structure, the knowledge obtained *a priori* serves as axioms or premises from which theoretical conclusions are deduced. The validation of these premises is of central importance in theory appraisal. In fact in Mises' view, the empirical and logical verification of premises and the confirmation of the soundness of the deductions based on these premises are the *only* elements in theory evaluation. Cairnes and John Neville Keynes also advocated the use of empirical observation to 'confirm' the products of deduction. In any case, the premises that serve as the logical foundation of theory are not arbitrary axioms under *a priorism*. They are treated as true statements. The use of premises as 'as if' hypotheticals is not consistent with this doctrine.

A priorism has been widely misunderstood and even misrepresented by its critics.[1] The recent revival of interest in the work of the so-called Austrian School of economists, and in the writings of Mises in particular, is redressing this imbalance.

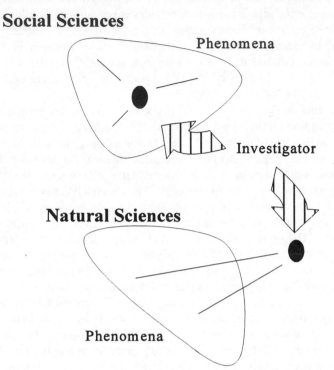

*Figure 6.1   The relationship between the investigator and phenomena in the
natural and the social sciences*

LIONEL ROBBINS

Lionel Robbins's (1932/1952) *Essay on the Nature and Significance of
Economic Science* is best known for providing the definition of economics
presented in most textbooks. Robbins challenged the traditional view that
economics was concerned about the discovery of the laws of the creation and
distribution of wealth. He suggested that economics should be seen as the
study of human behaviour as a relationship between ends and scarce means
that have alternative uses. But Robbins had more to say about the
methodology of economics than this contribution to the definition of the scope
of the discipline.

In the fourth chapter of the essay, Robbins explores the basis of the authority
of economic theory. Economic generalizations rest neither on induction from
regularities in historical data, nor on the results of controlled experiments.
Nevertheless, 'our belief in these propositions is as complete as belief based
upon any number of controlled experiments' (1932/1952, p. 75). The basis for

this confidence is what Robbins calls 'an elementary fact of experience' (1932/1952, p. 75) that people rank situations in term of preference. This elementary fact is an *a priori* axiom. The propositions of economic theory are deduced from such axioms, which are also described as 'assumptions involving in some way simple and indisputable facts of experience' (1932/1952, p. 78). According to Robbins, the main postulates include: for the theory of value, that individuals order situations in terms of their preferences; for the theory of production, that there is more than one factor of production; and for the theory of dynamics, that there is uncertainty regarding future scarcities. The *a priorist* position is that the test of validity for an *a priori* axiom is logical and introspective. In Robbins's words, 'These are not postulates the existence of whose counterpart in reality admits of extensive dispute once their nature is fully realised' (1932/1952, p. 79). Unlike the premises in mathematics or logic, the axioms of economics are not arbitrary. Therefore logically correct deductions from true premises are informative about the true nature of reality.

THE *A PRIORISM* OF MISES AND ROTHBARD

Two of the most vigorous exponents of *a priorism* in economics in the twentieth century were Ludwig von Mises and his student Murray Rothbard. Mises' views were developed in *Epistemological Problems of Economics*, published in translation in English in 1981 but originally published in German in 1933, in *The Ultimate Foundation of Economic Science*, published in 1962 and in his comprehensive treatise on economic theory, *Human Action*, published in 1949. Robbins acknowledged Mises specifically in the preface of his *Essay*.

Although Mises offered the most carefully reasoned statement of *a priorism*, he maintained that his views were essentially in the same tradition as J.S. Mill, Nassau Senior, J.E. Cairnes, John Neville Keynes and Carl Menger. According to this tradition, the goal of economic analysis was the understanding of the universal and essential nature of human action. The role of experience or observation was subordinate to reason in contributing to this understanding. Experience makes it possible to know the particular conditions of a specific action, but the general meaning of action is apprehended through reason. Economic inquiry begins with a short list of foundational axiomatic statements. These statements are universal and derived through reason based on understanding of the essential meaning of human action. They are not arbitrary, nor are they mere 'as if' propositions. Mises intends that these statements are verifiable. Mises never articulates an exhaustive list of these axioms. In *Epistemological Problems*, however, he does enumerate the 'fundamental categories of action' as action, economizing, preferring, the relationship between ends and means and 'everything else that, together with these, constitutes the system of human action' (1981, p. 13). The essential general meaning of action is that every human action is an attempt to substitute a more desired state for a less desired state. The need for economizing derives from the universal condition of scarcity. Preferring is necessary to give meaning to more and less desired states. Elsewhere, causality is included with these universal propositions, because action is undertaken because people believe, with some justification, that there is a relationship between actions and outcomes.

Mises maintains that these statements should not, and in fact cannot, be verified through observation alone. Mises occasionally, and the earlier *a priorists* frequently, refer to these axioms as self-evident, which has turned out to be an unfortunate choice of words. It has been interpreted by some to mean that validation of these statements is unimportant or even unnecessary. Nothing could be further from the truth. The test of validity is essential and demanding. The problem is that validation is not empirical, it is logical. The thing that qualifies these statements as valid *a priori* is that it is impossible for human beings to imagine their negation. In *The Ultimate Foundation*, Mises writes that 'The characteristic feature of *a priori* knowledge is that we cannot think of the truth of its negation or of something that would be at variance with it' (1978, p. 18), and 'In dealing with the *a priori* we are dealing with the mental tools that enable us to experience, to learn, to know and to act' (pp. 18, 19). Furthermore, any attempt to demonstrate that these axioms are false, in particular to contradict the idea that all human action is an attempt to substitute a more desired state for a less desired state, must of necessity involve an inconsistency, since such an attempt at refutation would itself constitute a purposeful human action. This fundamental axiom is treated as a nearly universal statement. It is not intended to apply to what Mises calls people in a 'vegetative state' where the role of the will in choice has been rendered ineffectual.

The structure of theory and the protocol for theory appraisal under *a priorism* is illustrated in Figure 6.2. Theory rests on these universal foundational axioms. The first step in theory appraisal is the validation of these statements. They are required to be true expressions of the essential nature of human action. Subsequent to the validation of these axioms, the economist adds statements about actual empirical conditions that are not necessarily universal. Mises and Rothbard as well as Robbins, refer to these statements as subsidiary axioms or limiting conditions. The validity of these statements is an empirical question. Either people are engaging in indirect exchange or they are not. Competition may be taking place, or it may not. Markets may be free or intervention in market exchange may be commonplace. The foundational axioms are used along with the relevant limiting conditions to deduce theorems. These conclusions are intended to correspond to phenomena in the external world. Contrary to some of the claims of his detractors, Mises does see a place for an empirical test of this correspondence.

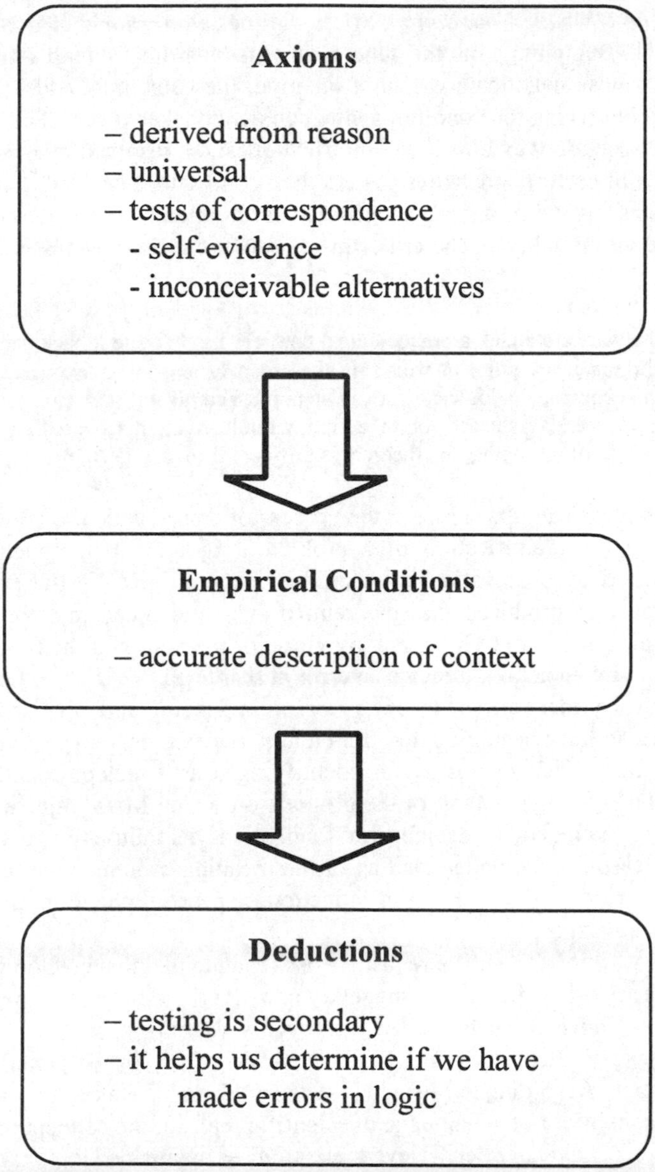

Axioms

– derived from reason
– universal
– tests of correspondence
  - self-evidence
  - inconceivable alternatives

Empirical Conditions

– accurate description of context

Deductions

– testing is secondary
– it helps us determine if we have
    made errors in logic

Figure 6.2 A priorist *theory appraisal*

In *The Ultimate Foundation*, Mises outlines an *a priorist* logic of theory appraisal. Beginning with the general axioms regarding human action, those axioms whose negation we cannot imagine, the economist adds subsidiary axioms concerning the conditions in which action takes place. The appraisal of these secondary axioms is an empirical question, resolved by observation. If the test of correspondence is passed, then conclusions derived jointly from the axioms and the empirically confirmed assumptions 'strictly describe what is going on in reality'. The criticism of theoretical conclusions proceeds as follows:

> He who wants to attack a praxeological theorem has to trace it back, step by step, until he reaches a point in which, in the chain of reasoning that resulted in the theorem concerned, a logical error can be unmasked. But if this regressive process of deduction ends at the category of action without having discovered a vicious link in the chain of reasoning, the theorem is fully confirmed. (1978, pp. 71, 72)

Observation can play a role in the process of theory validation, but only as an aid to the identification of a problem. If a theorem appears to be contradicted by observation, this could indicate an error in the process of deduction that produced that theorem, or it could mean that the limiting conditions do not hold. It cannot, by virtue of the nature of the fundamental axiom of human action, indicate an error at that level.

The most strident criticisms of *a priorism* in general, and of Mises's views in particular, have been mounted from a logical positivist perspective. Mises was an early critic of positivism, identifying it as a metaphysical doctrine (1978, pp. 116–17). Many of the grounds on which Mises rejected logical positivism, including its metaphysical foundations, its failure to appreciate the role of reason in the understanding of the meaning of human action, and its failure to resolve the problem of induction, appear prophetic in the light of recent scholarship.[2]

Mises was not a scientific realist. Mises maintained that economic theory was well served by the use of 'imaginary constructions'. An example of such a construction is what he called the 'evenly rotating economy', which in contemporary theory we might call an economy in perpetual general equilibrium. According to Mises, this state could not have a counterpart in any actual economy. In the language of scientific realism, the concept of general equilibrium could not refer.[3] Nevertheless, Mises maintained that this concept was a useful theoretical tool.

HOLLIS AND NELL – *A PRIORISM* AND RATIONALISM

Hollis and Nell (1975) also advocate an *a priorist* approach to economic methodology, although they use *a priorism* to defend a rationalist neo-Marxist position. They argue that neoclassical economic theory rests on a methodological foundation of empiricism or logical positivism. They judge this foundation to be unsound and conclude that the edifice of neoclassical theory is therefore precarious. Hollis and Nell present an important contemporary case study of *a priorism*. Robbins, Mises and Rothbard reached non-Marxist conclusions based on deduction from 'self-evident' axioms, so if Hollis and Nell have reached contradictory conclusions then this constitutes a serious problem for *a priorist* methodology.

Hollis and Nell begin by enumerating ten foundational methodological principles that they consider to be the mainstream neoclassical view. These ten tenets are listed in Table 6.1. This list has much in common with the one compiled by McCloskey. The Hollis and Nell list combines views identified elsewhere in this book as instrumentalism, especially as that doctrine has been articulated by Friedman (Tenet 8) and also includes empiricist ideas (Tenets 1, 3, 4, 5, 6, 9 and 10). Popperian falsification is present in Tenet 2 and a pragmatic solution to the problem of induction is suggested in Tenet 7. Hollis and Nell label this eclectic list as empiricism. While this compendium of views fails to recognize distinctions among competing methodological doctrines, I suspect that it corresponds closely to what a poll of economists would reveal as the consensus opinion on methodology in the profession.

The reader looking for the kind of painstaking development of methodological foundations undertaken by Mises will be disappointed by Hollis and Nell. The bulk of the book is devoted to criticism of 'empiricism' as an admixture of methodological views. The sixth chapter, '*A priori* Knowledge' and the seventh chapter, 'Deductive Explanation', contain the only sustained discussion of *a priorism* in the book. Chapter 6 contrasts the empiricist position regarding sources of knowledge with the 'rationalist' view. Unlike empiricists, rationalists affirm the possibility of *a priori* knowledge, that is, knowledge that is not the product of observation but that nevertheless conveys accurate knowledge about the external world. This means that *a priori* statements are more than just true by convention or mere tautologies. They, and deductions based on them, have empirical content. This erodes the empiricist's distinction between analytic and synthetic statements. The validation of *a priori* statements is logical. Although these statements are described by Hollis and Nell as self-evident, they really mean that *a priori* axioms cannot be denied without contradiction. All of this is a quite conventional enunciation of this methodological position. The departure from other twentieth century *a priorists* comes in Hollis and Nell's proposal for the fundamental axiom. They argue that what they call production, but what might be more correctly called reproduction, is the fundamental *a priori* axiom on which economic theory should be based. The notion of production that they invoke is defined as the conditions that must be met if a system, that is a social system, is to reproduce itself exactly. According to Hollis and Nell, it is necessary for an economy to reproduce the means of production perpetually.

Table 6.1 Hollis and Nell's ten tenets of neoclassical economics

---

1. Knowledge claims about the world can only be validated by experience.
2. Whatever is known by experience could have been otherwise.
3. Cognitively meaningful statements are either analytic or synthetic.
4. Synthetic statements cannot be known to be true *a priori*.
5. Analytic statements have no factual content.
6. Analytic statements are true by convention.
7. A causal law is a well-confirmed hypothesis.
8. Predictive success is the test of theory performance.
9. Value judgements have no place in science.
10. Sciences are distinguished by subject matter, not methodology.

Source: Hollis and Nell (1975, p. 10).

This necessity is presented as the fundamental axiom of economic theory. Unfortunately, this idea is offered as self-evident. No attempt is made to actually employ the logical apparatus required by *a priorism* to test the veracity of this proposed axiom. The reader is left to speculate why denial of this statement cannot be undertaken without contradiction. Unless the validation of this axiom is undertaken, deductions based on it do not have the claim of authority of conveying knowledge about the external world. The cognitive status of Hollis and Nell's theorems, therefore, remains uncertain. This resolves that apparent contradiction between the findings of Mises, Rothbard and Robbins on the one hand and Hollis and Nell on the other. *A priorism* is not a malleable methodological doctrine that can be used to support any view that an economist wants it to.

A PRIORISM AND THE FOUR KEY METHODOLOGICAL QUESTIONS

What is the Purpose of Economic Analysis?

Robbins, Mises and Rothbard, as well as Hollis and Nell, see the purpose of economic inquiry as improving understanding of human social interaction. *A priorists* are not optimistic about the prospects for quantitative prediction in economics. Some Austrian economists talk about pattern predictions. Some of these are qualitative. For example, if the

supply of money increases and the demand for money does not change, the
purchasing power of money will fall. These are predictions about general
tendencies that link causes and effects, and not predictions of actual outcomes.
Other pattern predictions relate to system performance. Mises and Hayek
predicted that a socialist economy would not be able to allocate the means of
production among alternative employments rationally. Hypothesis testing is
relegated to a secondary role in *a priorism*. If the consequences of the
fundamental axiom have been correctly deduced and the limiting conditions
are shown to hold, there is no role for empirical observation to play. Mises
does acknowledge that empirical hypothesis tests may be helpful in indicating
when deduction has not been performed correctly, but this is a far cry from the
function of the hypothesis test in instrumentalism or logical positivism.

What are the Sources of Economic Knowledge?

In contrast to empiricist methodologies such as logical positivism or
instrumentalism, *a priorism* affirms reason as an admissible source of
knowledge about economic phenomena. The insistence that the economist has
access to a source of knowledge about his subject that has no parallel in the
natural sciences is the driving force behind the notion of dualism. To Mises
and to Hollis and Nell, observation is a secondary source of knowledge to
reason.

Introspection or reason as a source of knowledge raises important issues of
validation. Many early *a priorists* appealed to 'self-evidence' in the validation
of *a priori* axioms. This created an impression of subjectivity that, to some,
appeared unscientific. Mises proposed an explicit logical test of the validity
of a statement that was put forward as an *a priori* axiom. A statement should
be accepted as valid if it was not possible to imagine circumstances in which
the statement did not hold. For example, the *a priori* characterization of
human action as an attempt to move from a less desirable state to a more
desirable state, according to Mises and Rothbard, passes this test. Even
attempts to imagine a situation in which it is not true affirm it.

A priorism does not resolve the problem of induction. Even Mises and
Rothbard acknowledge that the applicability of theorems derived from true *a
priori* axioms is limited to situations where the subsidiary axioms or empirical
conditions hold. How are we to determine when this is true? Mises's and
Rothbard's writings imply that this is a trivial task, but I am not convinced that
this is so.

What is the Scope of Economic Analysis?

Twentieth century *a priorists* are ambitious in defining the boundaries of
economic analysis. To Mises, all human action outside of human beings in a
vegetative state is within the scope of praxeological analysis. Hollis and Nell

are less clear, but if we accept their fundamental axiom of the necessity of the reproduction of the means of production, then anything related to that process could be included within economics. Lionel Robbins is the most circumspect of the twentieth century *a priorists*. His definition of economics as the study of the allocation of scarce means among competing ends delimits the boundaries of economics to the rational realm. If either ends or means are uncertain, in the Knightian sense, then action falls in the non-rational category. Israel Kirzner's studies of entrepreneurship, if we followed Robbins's definition strictly, would not qualify as economics.

A priorists are generally cautious about the prospects for quantitative prediction in economics. In the absence of empirical constants, prediction is problematical. Neither parameters nor variables can be treated as constants for the purposes of prediction.

What is the Appropriate Structure of an Economic Theory?

Economic theory is deductive in *a priorism*. As indicated above, theory is deduced from validated true premises. The first component in any theory is the validation of these premises. Hollis and Nell treat their premise, the reproduction of the means of production, as self-evident. No protocol for validation is articulated. Mises, on the other hand, is explicit regarding premise validation. His test is logical. He contends that the validity of the premise that every human action is an attempt to move from a less desired state to a more desired one is established by the fact that it is impossible for us to conceive of human existence if it is not true. *A priorists* in the Austrian tradition have been critical of the use of mathematics in economic reasoning. This criticism is based, in part, on the distinction between rational and teleological behaviour. Non-Austrian neoclassical economists characterize human behaviour as rational, in the sense of being consistent with some well-structured set of preferences. This notion of rationality lends itself to mathematical representation as a constrained optimization problem. Teleological behaviour is behaviour directed towards the achievement of ends. It does not necessarily require consistency with a set of stable well-structured preferences. Ends may change, as may perceptions about opportunities. Teleological behaviour is not readily represented as the solution to a constrained maximization problem.

CRITICS OF *A PRIORISM*

Several influential economists have been outspoken critics of the *a priorist* position. Hutchison, Samuelson and Blaug, all of whom have advocated some sort of Popperian empiricism, have flatly rejected *a priorism* as 'unscientific'. This seems to mean that it does adhere to the logical positivist and falsificationist view of science. Hutchison was an early critic of the *a priorist* approach. He chides economists holding *a priorist* views that they have been unable to compile a generally accepted list of propositions derived from introspection. Mises and Robbins have presented lists of *a priori* axioms, but these lists are not completely consistent and neither of these authors claims that his list is exhaustive. Hutchison suggests that such a list should include the maximum principle, the law of diminishing marginal utility and the principle of scarcity.

Hutchison (1981) challenges advocates of *a priorism* on two fronts: clarify the meaning and scope of applicability of these propositions and indicate how they can be tested 'in a scientifically respectable way' (p. 136). In particular, he wants to know how introspective and subjective personal knowledge can be transformed into objective knowledge that pertains to other people. He also raises the prospect of self-serving or even delusional introspection. He concludes

> No scientist can rely on introspection alone if he wants results of general applicability ... Though on the other hand, he could conceivably, if scarcely in practice, dispense with introspection entirely, it is certainly an invaluable and in fact practically indispensable method for the forming of general hypotheses about one's fellow human beings ... though all such hypotheses must afterwards be tested by empirical investigation. (pp. 142–3)

Although Gerrard argues that *a priorism,* or at least deductivism, is the most influential methodological doctrine in economics today, the views of Mises have generally been rejected. As Caldwell has cogently argued, however, much of the criticism directed at Mises has been based on a less than careful reading of what he actually said. A noteworthy example is Hutchison (1981, p. 223) who goes so far as to link Mises's methodological position with anti-libertarian totalitarianism. Anyone with even a casual familiarity with Mises's writings on economic policy will be either amused or appalled by him being described as an enemy of freedom. Readers who take the time to assimilate key definitions and distinctions find Mises's views less controversial.

Samuelson's rejection of *a priorism* and Blaug's position, which is derived from Samuelson's, are disappointingly superficial. Invoking the name of Thomas Jefferson and drawing a parallel between Jefferson's aversion to slavery and his own aversion to *a priorist* methodological reasoning, Samuelson expresses astonishment that these views could ever have been taken seriously. But this is not the stuff of sustained critical analysis. Like Hutchison, Blaug and Samuelson seem unable to see beyond a narrow interpretation of Popperian empiricism. They also fail to appreciate the combined combination of introspective on empirical process of theory appraisal required by rigorous *a priorism*. Neither Robbins nor Mises advocated that introspection was the exclusive source of knowledge for economic theorists. But this subtlety seems to have been lost on the leading critics.

A priorism is a coherent methodological position that makes strong claims about the validity of the theorems that can be derived from true axioms. That it has been passed by in methodological discourse in economics, often for reasons that are not compelling, is beside the point. The fatal limitation of *a priorism* is that it frustrates the predictive ambitions of economists. The attraction of the rationality postulate is that it produces less equivocal predictions than Mises's fundamental axiom of action. If economists are convinced that the road to scientific credibility is paved with the stones of unambiguous quantitative predictions, then they will have little interest in *a priorism*.

QUESTIONS FOR DISCUSSION

1. Do you agree with Gerrard that deductivism is the most influential methodological doctrine in economics?
2. How does the *a priorism* of Mises compare to that of Hollis and Nell?
3. Evaluate the arguments advanced by the critics of *a priorism*.
4. Is neoclassical economics built exclusively on a foundation of logical positivism?

NOTES

1. For an example, see Blaug (1992, pp. 81–2).
2. Daniel Hausman's *The Inexact and Separate Science of Economics* and Alexander Rosenberg's *Economics – Mathematical Politics or Science of Diminishing Returns?* both claim that economics is somehow different from the natural sciences and that prediction is problematical in economics. Neither of these authors acknowledges Mises's contributions to these ideas, but these independent conclusions may rehabilitate Mises's tarnished reputation with many economists.
3. See Chapter 7 for a description of scientific realism.

7. Economics as Realism

INTRODUCTION

This chapter describes a methodological viewpoint known as scientific realism. This is one of the more important methodological positions in the philosophy of science, but it has few followers among economists.

Scientific realism is an old theory of knowledge which has recently experienced a renaissance among methodologists.[1] The content of scientific realism can be summarized in five propositions: independence, apprehension, reference, linearity and truthfulness.

Independence

Phenomena in the world are held to be independent of consciousness of the investigator. Things have real existence. According to Bhaskar (1975, p. 27) 'if there were no science, there would still be a nature, and it is this nature which is investigated by science'.

Independence implies that the agenda for scientific inquiry is set, ultimately, by phenomena. Assessment of a scientific theory should be based on the degree to which that theory explicates the nature of phenomena. The independence proposition does not necessarily rule out the study of hypothetical situations as an expositional aid or as part of the process of deduction, but scientific realist views on independence and reference require a clear link between the investigation of hypothetical cases and the phenomena being analysed.

Apprehension

Reality, in its independent existence, can be perceived and understood by the patient and clever investigator. Feyerabend (1981) maintains that scientific inquiry is the best available means to explore and understand the world, but he offers this proposition without argumentation. Apprehension is not unique to scientific realism. Instrumentalist economists who seek only useful predictions from theories must also maintain that investigators can perceive and understand what is being predicted.

Reference

The semantic content of scientific realism is one of its most emphasized elements. According to Hooker, the reference thesis asserts that 'if a scientific theory is in fact true, then there is in the world exactly those entities which the theory says there is, having exactly these characteristics which the terms of the theory describe them as having' (1987, p. 7). Elements of a theory refer to real entities which have independent existence. Reference therefore combines the ideas of independence of phenomena and the relevance of truthfulness in the appraisal of theory. It also provides guidance for the practice of scientific inquiry. Efforts to eliminate non-referential elements from existing theories are progressive.

Linearity

Scientific realism offers an explanation of the progress of scientific inquiry. This progress is characterized as sequential and linear. New theories build on old theories. Old theories turn out to be limiting cases of new theories. New theories, in addition to explaining and predicting phenomena, explain the shortcomings of old theories. Progress in science consists of successively more accurate approximations of real processes, structures or phenomena. Boyd (1983) has suggested that this progress may in fact take place dialectically. A corollary of the linearity hypothesis is that concepts and terms can be compared across paradigms and over the schisms of scientific revolutions, in contrast to Kuhn (1970) who rejected the possibility of this type of semantic continuity.

Truthfulness

Scientific realism invokes truthfulness as an appropriate criterion for the appraisal of theory. This is an important point to emphasize in discussions of the methodology of economics, which has been influenced by an instrumentalist view that truthfulness of a theory is irrelevant or impossible to assess and that 'usefulness' is a more appropriate standard.

Hooker (1987) admits that there can be no independent validation of truthfulness, that no actual theory can be known to be true, but that theories are nevertheless intended to be true representations. Present theories should therefore be treated with an attitude of scepticism. The truthfulness criterion embodies a motivational aspect of scientific realism. Feyerabend (1981) concludes that many prominent natural scientists, including Einstein, expressed this motivation in their writings on methodology.

In emphasizing the role of theory as explanation of real phenomena, scientific realism embraces a brand of essentialism. This is particularly evident in Feyerabend's discussion.

REALISM AND THE FOUR KEY METHODOLOGICAL QUESTIONS

What is the Purpose of Economic Analysis?

A scientific realist maintains that 'Science aims to give us, in its theories, a literally true story of what the world is like' (van Fraassen, 1980, p. 24). The realist accepts the external world as existing independently of human thought or observation. With regard to the interpretation of theories, to the realist, central terms refer to actual independently existing entities, both observable and unobservable. A realist interprets scientific progress as the evolution of theories to obtain more and more accurate approximations of true independent reality and as the acceptance of new theories which subsume old theories as special cases.

Lawson (1992) argues that the aim of the scientific realist economist is more than prediction. The goal of science is to identify and to understand the relationships between causes and effects that express themselves in general tendencies but not necessarily in particular outcomes in events. This places the aim of scientific economics closer to the understanding view than what I described as the explanation and prediction model in Chapter 3.

What are the Sources of Economic Knowledge?

If Lawson (1989) and Maki (1989, 1990) are correct in interpreting Keynes, Simon and Kirzner as scientific realists, then this methodology would seem to admit reason as a source of knowledge in economic science. Each of these writers draws logical inferences from definitions and from general axioms that are intended to convey substantive knowledge about reality. So scientific realism is not an exclusively empiricist methodology. Realists' insistence that even theoretical terms for unobservable entities in a theory refer, intimates that an exclusive reliance on observation is not consistent with realism. Realists vary in their insistence on the reference of non-observables in theories.

What is the Scope of Economic Analysis?

According to Maki (1989, 1990), Simon and Kirzner invoke a broader notion of rationality in the economic analysis of human behaviour. Simon proposes an alternative to the maximizing view of rationality, and Kirzner's treatment of entrepreneurship is intentionally outside the scope of application of the idea of rationality at least as that term is used in neoclassical economic theory. The primacy of reference of theoretical terms has important implications for priorities in economic research. Theories that do not refer should be modified or replaced with theories that do. But so far, scientific realist economists have been primarily concerned with theory appraisal and have not overly concerned themselves with the implications of scientific realism on delimiting the scope of economic inquiry.

What is the Structure of Economic Theory?

The concept of reference, the hallmark feature of realism, has implications for the interpretation of theory. Every element of a theory should refer. Even the unobservable elements of a theory refer to real entities, or to actual properties of real entities. Under scientific realism, Debreu's description of the axioms of consumer theory (1959, p. 52), listed in decreasing order of plausibility, is a revealing confession. The theory does not refer. Its axioms are arbitrary. To the realist, this reveals a fatal flaw. In fact, the entire elegant theory of the existence of competitive equilibrium and the welfare properties associated with that equilibrium, appear peculiar through the lenses of scientific realism. It is not the aim of this chapter to offer a definitive appraisal of the validity of scientific realism.[2] Nevertheless, an overview of some of the arguments for and against this theory of knowledge is helpful. Proponents of scientific realism frequently claim that, as Putnam said, 'it is only philosophy that doesn't make the success of science a miracle' (quoted in Laudan).

If scientific theories were not at least approximately true and becoming closer in their approximation to truth, what accounts for the contribution of scientific discovery to technological advance? Of course, this argument is not definitive. It merely challenges opponents to develop a better alternative. Perhaps one day they will. Scientific realism clearly contradicts Kuhn's view on the non-comparability of terms across paradigms and the instrumentalists' rejection of truthfulness in theory appraisal. Laudan suggests that there is vagueness and a certain logical circularity in scientific realism, but his critique ends with this:

> All of us would like realism to be true; we would like to think that science works because it has got a grip on how things really are. But such claims have yet to be made out. Given the present status of this fact, it can only be wish fulfilment that gives rise to the claim that realism, and realism alone, explains why science works. (1981, p. 242)

Scientific realism would appear to face formidable obstacles as a theory of economic epistemology. The subjective theory of value and the participant observer effect blur the distinction between human consciousness and independent phenomena. Radical subjectivists such as Lachmann argue that there are no underlying independent economic realities. Perception is reality. The participant observer effect can occur in several ways. If an economist discovers a way to forecast prices and acts on the basis of that knowledge, the theory embodied in the forecast may be rendered invalid, even though it may have been a truthful representation of actual processes and structures before the investigator acted. The problem of observational equivalence, discussed at length by Boyd (1983) with reference to the natural sciences, is a hallmark of work in the New Classical Macroeconomics tradition. How are two observationally equivalent theories to be assessed as representations of a presumably unitary independent real phenomenon?

The linearity hypothesis would appear to be contradicted by the history of thought in economics. As Blaug has observed, old economic theories never seem to die. There seems, for example, to be a Kondratieff wave of Kondratieff wave theories (see Marshall, 1987 and Fox, 1988). As Lavoie (1985) has observed, both sides of the famous 'Socialist Calculation Debate' of the 1920s and 1930s continue to claim victory, often appealing to the same data. Lavoie, however, provides corroboration of the position that translation of terms across paradigms, while problematical, can be achieved.

REALISM IN THE METHODOLOGY OF ECONOMICS

Realism as an epistemological and methodological doctrine has suffered alternately from neglect and abuse by economists. To the extent that 'realism' is discussed by economic theorists or economic methodologists, all too often the emphasis is on the 'realism of assumptions' debate in the 1940s and 1950s and on Friedman's essay. It is hardly surprising, given this context, that many economists look awry at arguments being made from a scientific realist perspective.

Machlup is typical of the views on realism held by economists at mid-century. He views realism and abstraction as two ends of a continuum related to the characteristics of a model. To Machlup, realism is synonymous with cluttering up a model with irrelevant details. In his words, 'people who are superficial who prefer to "look" rather than to "think" and are more interested in the outer trappings than in the inner workings of things are wont to complain about models that are "unrealistic"' (1978, p. 78). Machlup also suggests that realism and relevance are incompatible ends in the development of economic theory (p. 187).

Blaug (1980, 1992), in his five chapter overview of the methodology of economics does not mention scientific realism. His references to 'realism' are in the context of the realism of assumptions debate and reaction to Friedman's essay. McCloskey does not address scientific realism either in his book or in his influential paper (1983, 1985). In an exchange with Maki (1988), however, McCloskey (1988) claims to be a realist and argues that his study of the rhetoric of economics is an expression of scientific realism. Maki's response to McCloskey conveys scepticism regarding the relationship between McCloskey's position and scientific realism. Part of the problem is that McCloskey does not actually say what he means by realism. Lawrence Boland (1982, 1989) is also silent on the subject of scientific realism. He does address the 'realism of assumptions' debate, but like many other economic methodologists fails to distinguish between realism of assumptions and realism as a methodological position. Klant (1984) also does not discuss scientific realism.

Hausman does discuss scientific realism and explores its relationship to the methodology of economics (Hausman (ed.), 1984, Introduction and 1992, Appendix). He maintains that scientific realism and instrumentalism are the two main schools of thought among philosophers of science regarding the goals of science. According to Hausman, scientific realists maintain that science should help us discover new truths about the world and to explain in addition to enabling us to make successful predictions. Hausman's discussion acknowledges that while realism maintains that theories are true representations of real objects and phenomena, that the state of human knowledge at a point in time is subject to error and that theories as a consequence are subject to revision and correction.

Caldwell (1982) argues that most contemporary philosophers of science have adopted some view of scientific realism. He fails to address the obvious question of why the views of scientific realism have had such limited impact on the thinking of methodologists of economics. Much of his discussion of realism dwells on the use of the term popularized by Friedman's essay. Nevertheless, Caldwell and Hausman represent the high water mark for discussions of scientific realism among the methodologists of economics, at least until the publication of recent papers by Maki (1989, 1990) and Lawson (1989, 1992) refocused economists' thinking on the subject. In Maki's view, the so-called realism of assumptions debate was misnamed. At issue was the function and purpose of abstraction in economic theory. Maki characterizes this as the 'realisticness' of assumptions but semantic confusion might be reduced if the more traditional categories of abstraction versus concreteness were maintained. At issue then, in the infamous debate in the 1940s and 1950s, was the proper level of abstractness versus concreteness in the assumptions used in economic theory. Maki has identified realist themes in the work of Menger and certain members of the Austrian School, including Israel Kirzner, as well as in the work of Herbert Simon.

Lawson (1989), following the characterization of scientific realism outlined by Bhaskar (1975), interprets Keynes's (1939) critique of the research programme in econometrics in terms of the tension between realism and instrumentalism. Lawson's realist perspective on economics contends that explanation, not prediction, is the purpose of economic analysis. Economists need to be content articulating general tendencies of economic systems, because quantitative predictions of specific events are outside the realm of the possible. Lawson (1992) also interprets Friedman's position as instrumentalism.

Scientific realism needs to be seen as an alternative to and not necessarily compatible with the more familiar doctrines of logical positivism and instrumentalism which dominate current thinking on methodology by economists. Clouded by the regrettable legacy of the realism of assumptions debate, discussions of scientific realism frequently sound archaic to modern economists. Recent work by philosophers of science on the appraisal and evolution of the ideas of scientific realism have been taken up relatively slowly by economists. Nevertheless, as Lawson and Maki have shown, scientific realism has been an important theme in the work of some economists even though the ideas of realism have not been made explicit. It is my contention that Ronald Coase has pursued a realist research agenda and that his writings reflect this pursuit in heretofore unappreciated ways.

RONALD COASE AS A SCIENTIFIC REALIST

It is possible that more words have been written about Ronald Coase than have been written by him. Many of his contributions have continued to have substantial influence long after their initial publication. Steven Cheung (1983) has suggested that this influence has grown exponentially with time but this is true only of his two most famous essays (see Table 7.1). Coase attributes much of the controversy surrounding his writing to his difficulty in putting his ideas into words. My view is that an important contributing factor to the polemical reaction to Coase arises from his views on the methodology of economics. Coase's views conform closely to scientific realism.

This is not to say that Coase is an overt realist. His explicitly methodological works are few and he does not offer a description of or a name for his position. Furthermore, it is not possible, based on Coase's writings, to ascertain his views on all of the theses considered to comprise the realist view. Notwithstanding this ambiguity, I will contend that what are arguably Coase's most influential contributions, his recognition of the existence and importance of transaction costs in market exchange and his insistence on the importance of law as an institution regulating exchange, are expressions of a realist orientation to economic inquiry

On more than one occasion, Coase has denied any claim to authority as a methodologist. In his 1982 Nutter lecture, he protests 'I should add that I am in no sense well informed in the philosophy of science. Words like epistemology do not come tripping from my tongue' (1982, p. 6). Nevertheless, Coase speaks on the subject of methodology often. In the first chapter of *The Firm, the Market and the Law,* Coase writes '[it] would seem to imply that most economists have a different way of looking at economic problems and do not share my conception of the nature of our subject' (1988a, p. 1). Characterization of the nature and purpose of inquiry of a particular field is clearly a question of methodology, and Coase sees himself as a dissenting voice. In particular, he questions the fruitfulness of following Robbins's notion that economics is the study of allocation of limited means among competing ends. This definition, which emphasizes the formal logic

Table 7.1 Citation counts of selected articles by Ronald Coase, 1956–1990

Article	1956–1965	1966–1970	1971–1975	1976–1980	1981–1985	1986–1990
'The Nature of the Firm' (1937)	15	16	47	114	212	346
'The Marginal Cost Controversy' (1946)	3	5	8	5	12	13
'The Federal Communications Commission' (1959)	20	26	33	35	37	43
'The Problem of Social Cost' (1960)	17	88	241	347	566	451
'The Independent Radio Advisory Committee' (1962)	0	13	2	3	2	2
'The Theory of Public Utility Pricing and Its Application' (1970)	–	0	19	10	4	2
'Durability and Monopoly' (1972)	–	–	5	12	13	44
'The Lighthouse in Economics' (1974)	–	–	3	12	17	27
'The Market for Goods and the Market for Ideas' (1974)	–	–	1	14	10	12
'Advertising and Free Speech' (1977)	–	–	–	14	6	15
'The Coase Theorem and the Empty Core: A Comment' (1981)	–	–	–	–	8	21

Source: Social Sciences Citation Index

of optimization and choice, 'has nevertheless had, in my view, serious adverse effects on economics itself' (Coase, 1988a, p. 3).

This adverse effect has been the neglect of the study of the institutional settings in which choice and exchange take place. By suggesting that economics may be more than the formal logic of optimization, Coase shows some sympathy for Buchanan (1964), but more important in the present context, he reveals himself as a closet methodologist. Several of Coase's most influential and controversial papers use realist arguments. His own exposition of the meaning and significance of his own work is clearly in the scientific realist tradition. Coase is often sharply critical of the state of economic theory. He repeatedly emphasizes three principles that have been violated in economic research. First, theory is subservient to phenomena. The so-called real world is not a special case. Second, he repeatedly emphasizes the need for economists to study the action of actual agents in the context of existing institutions as part of the development and validation of theory. Finally, Coasian methodology erases the traditional and revered distinction (see Leijonhufvud, 1973) between 'theoretical' and 'applied' research.

The most obviously realist element is Coase's insistence on the reference of theoretical terms. This reference is combined with an emphasis on the independent existence of phenomena. Firms exist. Transaction costs exist. Lighthouses exist. Markets exist. Independent existence of phenomena is behind the entreaty to investigate the nature of those real entities identified as elements in theories. It also motivates the proposition that the existence of real entities (transaction costs), should influence the configuration of theoretical analysis (welfare economics).

Coase's contributions to economic theory focus on public utility pricing and management, welfare economics and law and economics. In this last area, his work has emphasized the relationships between legal rights and exchange. Reference serves as a unifying theme of contributions in each of these areas. Much of Coase's criticism of economic theory derives from concern for reference. Some examples of this critique include

> The rational utility maximizer bears no resemblance to the man on the Clapham bus or, indeed, to any man (or woman) on any bus. There is no reason to suppose that most human beings are engaged in maximizing anything unless it be unhappiness, and even this with incomplete success. (1988a, p. 3)

regarding 'The Problem of Social Cost': 'What my argument does suggest is the need to introduce positive transactions costs explicitly into economic analysis so that we can study the world that exists. This has not been the effect of my article' (1988a, p. 15). Regarding the analysis of external affects inherited from Pigou:

> [H]e did not make any detailed studies of the working of economic institutions ... the situation in which sparks from a railway locomotive could start fires which burnt

> woods on land adjoining the railway without the railway having to pay compensation
> to the owners of the woods ... had come about not because of lack of governmental
> action but in consequence of it.
>
> Modern economists, in the main, use the same approach as Pigou, although with
> some change in terminology and even greater detachment from the real world.
> (1988a, pp. 22, 23)

Finally, from his Nutter Lecture, 'most of us would not value the theory if we
did not think these implications corresponded to happenings in the real
economic system' (1982, p. 6) and 'Realism in assumptions forces us to
analyze the world that exists not some imaginary world that does not' (1982,
p. 7).

Reference also motivated 'The Nature of the Firm' in which Coase hopes to
show 'that a definition of a firm may be obtained which is not only realistic in
that it corresponds to what is meant by a firm in the real world, but is tractable'
(1937/1988, p. 34).   The need for such a definition derives from Coase's
characterization of the purpose for an economic theory of the firm.   This
purpose is to provide answers to three questions:

1.   Why do firms exist?
2.   What determines the number of firms?
3.   What determines what firms do? (for example, what inputs they buy and
     what outputs they sell).

These are not the central questions addressed by the theory of production in
contemporary microeconomics (see Machlup, 1978, Chapter 16, and
Henderson and Quandt, 1980, Chapter 4).

According to Coase, the firm is an organization in which market transactions
are replaced by entrepreneurial direction and in which production is
undertaken.   The distinguishing mark of the firm is the suppression of the price
mechanism in favour of direct coordination.   The explanation for the existence
of firms focuses on transaction costs.   The size of a firm is determined by
balancing the costs of transacting against the costs of entrepreneurial direction.
The costs of entrepreneurial direction include failures by entrepreneurs to
direct factors of production to their most productive employment and the cost
of administration.   Having offered this explanation and definition of the firm,
Coase proceeds to ascertain 'whether the concept of the firm which has been
developed fits in with that existing in the real world' (1937/1988, p. 53).   He
proceeds to an analysis of legal aspects of employer/employee relationships
and other contractual relations in firms.

Why is this scientific realism?   First, the institutions called firms are treated
as having real and independent existence.   The purpose of the theory
articulated by Coase is to explain the emergence and evolution of these
institutions.   Second, terms used in the theory are referential.   There is a

correspondence between the language of the theory and the known institutions described as firms which have existence in the world. Even the title of Coase's paper reflects a brand of essentialism which is frequently characteristic of scientific realism.

Coase's early work on the hog cycle with R.F. Fowler (1935a, 1935b, 1937, 1940) also exhibits themes of scientific realism. The contemporary reader might be put off by the painstaking study of the actual technology, management and biology of hog production which is undertaken in these papers. Commitment to the study of actual phenomena leads Coase and Fowler to question whether it is correct to describe historical fluctuations in hog prices and production as being a 'cycle' at all, given that the data exhibit neither a constant period nor amplitude. It is clearly consistent with scientific realism that the final paper in this series, which addresses the general problem of a theory of producer expectations, is the culmination of the study of a particular existing situation. Elements in the theory of producers' expectations are intended to be referential.

Coase and Fowler affirm the truthfulness thesis of scientific realism as well. They repeatedly indicate the need for verification of a theory, making them at the very least not instrumentalists. Their assessment of the cobweb model as an explanation of the UK hog cycle is more telling. Their rejection of that model is based on a test of the model's assumptions regarding producers' expectations. They argue that the assumption of constant expectations on the part of producers is at variance with objective observations of phenomena and conclude that the model therefore cannot be offered as an explanation of cyclical variations in prices and production.

'The Marginal Cost Controversy' (1946/1988) constitutes a critique of the Hotelling and Lerner model of optimal pricing under decreasing average costs. The standard solution for efficient pricing under such a regime is to choose output so as to equate price and marginal cost and then to use tax revenues to subsidize the difference between average cost and price on that optimal output. Coase's critique draws on a number of realist themes. He insists on examining the nature of actual phenomena as opposed to the formal properties of hypothetical situations. The second section of the paper begins

> Any actual economic situation is complex and a single economic problem does not exist in isolation. Consequently, confusion is liable to result because economists dealing with an actual situation are attempting to solve several problems at once. I believe this is true of the question I am discussing in this article. The central problem relates to a divergence between average and marginal costs. But in any actual case two other problems usually arise. (1946/1988, p. 77)

This brief portion of text emphasizes both the independence of the existence of economic phenomena and the necessity of the examination of actual economic situations. Unravelling complex economic phenomena leads Coase to the argument for multi-part pricing as a solution to situations apparently characterized by decreasing average costs.

'The Federal Communications Commission' (1959), like his later contribution 'The Lighthouse in Economics' (1974b), shows Coase's commitment to the careful examination of actual situations as the raw material of theoretical insights. It was in his 1959 paper that Coase began to develop the relationships among transaction costs, property rights, and market failure which he was to develop more fully in 'The Problem of Social Cost'. A careful review of technical documents and policy decisions from the beginning of the century is used to illustrate that the conventional wisdom, as of 1959 at least, was that broadcasting was either a natural monopoly or an activity which of necessity had to be provided by the state. Quoting Siepmann, 'Private enterprise, over seven long years, failed to set its own house in order. Cut throat competition at once retarded radio's orderly development and subjected listeners to intolerable strain and inconvenience' (see Coase, 1959, p. 13). Coase continues in his essentialist bent by claiming that the views of Siepmann were based on a misunderstanding of the nature of the problems involved in broadcasting. Rather than concluding that broadcasting is inevitably a natural monopoly or a service which could only be provided by the state, Coase suggests that the cause of the problem is that property rights in radio frequencies were prevented from emerging. As in 'The Marginal Cost Controversy', Coase elects to examine the problems of natural monopoly and public provision of services by carefully examining an actual case in an effort to uncover the underlying factors which create a situation which cannot be addressed by voluntary exchange in markets.

In what is arguably his most famous paper, 'The Problem of Social Cost' (1960) and in the companion piece 'Notes on the Problem of Social Cost' (1988b), Coase adopts his strongest scientific realist position. This study addresses the nature, origin and consequences of actions undertaken by business firms which have non-contractual, non-pecuniary effects on other parties. Throughout the paper, the concept of the firm is clearly referential. Extending the notion of transaction costs introduced in 'The Nature of the Firm', Coase argues that these costs exist and have real effects on the outcomes of contractual and exchange relations. Throughout the paper, the need to understand actual situations and the use of theory as a tool in obtaining understanding of actual situations is re-emphasized. For example,

> Satisfactory views on policy can only come from a patient study of how, in practice, the market, firms and governments handle the problem of external effects ... (1960/1988, p. 118)

> The problem is to define practical arrangements which will correct defects in one part of the system without creating more serious harm in other parts. (1960/1988, p. 142)

Start our analysis with a situation approximating that which actually exists ... (1960/1988, p. 154)

In 'Notes on the Problem of Social Cost' Coase (1988b) argues that it is precisely the real existence of transaction costs and the real consequences of those costs which represents the point of departure for his study of external effects from work in the tradition of Pigou. He characterizes modern economic theory as a theory of a world of zero transaction costs. This is seen as a fatal limitation. In the first chapter of *The Firm, the Market and the Law* Coase explains 'In an economic theory which assumes that transactions costs are nonexistent, markets have no functions to perform' (1988, p. 7) and 'What my argument does suggest is the need to introduce positive transactions costs into the analysis so that we can study the world that exists' (1988, p. 15). The assumption of zero transaction costs is incompatible with the persistent existence of unrealized gains from exchange which enduring externalities represent.[3] Coase offers a scientific realist critique of modern welfare and environmental economics. Coase makes some effort to distance himself from the so-called 'Coase Theorem' in his 'Notes'. One gets the impression that Coase regrets the extended and at times animated discussions which followed the publication of the paper, and that much of this discussion has reduced the impact of what Coase really intended us to understand from 'The Problem of Social Cost'.

'The Lighthouse in Economics' (1974/1988), concludes by asking how so many great economists could have been so wrong for so long regarding the characterization of the nature of services from lighthouses as an example of a so-called public good. As in the case of 'The Federal Communications Commission', Coase, motivated by the writings of John Stuart Mill, Henry Sidgwick, A.C. Pigou and Paul Samuelson, examined the origins and evolution of the lighthouse industry in Britain. The purpose of this examination was to consider whether this industry was subject to the types of incentive problems described in economics textbooks. Prior to Coase, no economist had made a careful study of the actual operation of the lighthouse industry. In 'The Lighthouse', 'lighthouses' are referential. By showing that lighthouses came into existence and operated successfully on a self-sustaining financial basis, Coase demonstrates that when 'the lighthouse is simply plucked out of the air to serve as an illustration' (1974/1988, p. 211), abstract economic analysis takes on a misleading veneer of concreteness and can lead economists to see problems which do not in fact exist. For example, using historical records, Coase was able to find examples in which entrepreneurs were able to make more than a reasonable living in the provision of lighthouse services. Coase concludes his critique of the conventional treatment of lighthouses by saying 'such generalizations are not likely to be helpful unless they are derived from studies of how such activities are actually carried out within different institutional frameworks' (1974/1988, p. 211). This type of investigation has been a hallmark of Coase's published work.   According to Landes *et al.* (1983), he also encouraged colleagues at the University of Chicago and contributors to the *Journal of Law and Economics* to study how 'markets actually worked'.   The steadfast insistence that pig producers, firms, transaction costs, laws, state-owned enterprises and lighthouses exist and that an important goal of economic research is to contribute to our understanding of the nature and significance of that existence, exemplifies a scientific realist approach to economic inquiry.   In the brief essay 'Marshall on Method' (1975), Coase describes Marshall's belief that economists should not study 'imaginary problems not conforming to the conditions of real life' (p. 31) with much sympathy.   His tone in posing the rhetorical question 'Do we concern ourselves not with puzzles presented by the real economic world but with the puzzles presented by other economists' analysis?' (p. 31) indicates that he would answer in the affirmative.

Coase's position on the linearity thesis of scientific realism, however, is at best equivocal.   Linearity offers an explanation of the success of science. Professor Coase is loath to acknowledge much success in contemporary economics.   According to Dingle (1980), Coase feels that no contemporary book on economics will be remembered in 50 years.   He frequently despairs in *The Firm, the Market and the Law* of the limited and generally unproductive influence that 'The Nature of the Firm' and 'On the Problem of Social Cost' have had on the economics profession.   The apparent difficulty in absorbing the concept of transaction costs into modern price theory contradicts the idea of new theories being built on old ones.   There is, nevertheless, some evidence of the linearity thesis in some of Coase's work.   In 'The Lighthouse' and 'Social Cost' he takes pains to trace the intellectual roots of his analysis.   In each of these contributions, however, his intent is to illuminate error and inconsistency in the received view.   This is consistent with Boyd's (1983) dialectical characterization of linearity, but given Coase's frequent expressions of frustration with the state of contemporary economic theory, it is difficult to conclude that he sees much movement along the vector of progress.

CONCLUSIONS

Throughout his published work, Coase has consistently treated economic phenomena as having independent real existence.   He has treated elements of economic theory, such as 'firms', as referential.   When real phenomena, such as transaction costs, are conspicuous by their absence from economic theory, Coase, as a scientific realist, calls for their incorporation into theory.   But scientific realism is a minority view in economic methodology.   And Friedman's essay has been an impediment to economists' understanding of realism as a methodological doctrine.   As a result, Coase has been controversial, not because he has had difficulty in putting his ideas into words, but because his views on the methodology of economics represent a minority view.

QUESTIONS FOR DISCUSSION

1. Compare scientific realism with the position on the realism of assumptions that Milton Friedman rejects.
2. Do you agree with Ronald Coase that no contemporary book in economics will be remembered in 50 years?
3. Make a list of issues on which scientific realists and instrumentalists disagree. On what issues do they agree?

NOTES

1. The interested reader is referred to Perry (1912), Evans (1928), Sellars (1966), Feyerabend (1981), Hooker (1987), Bhaskar (1975) and Boyd (1983).
2. Boyd (1983) and Laudan (1981) provide an introduction to this task.
3. See Cheung (1978) for further development of this point.

8. Economics as Conversation and Rhetoric

INTRODUCTION

Donald McCloskey has emerged as an influential critic of mainstream methodology in economics. Beginning with the publication of his essay 'The Rhetoric of Economics' in the *Journal of Economic Literature* in 1983, followed by his book of the same title two years later, McCloskey has raised the profile of rhetorical analysis among economists. One of the aims of the rhetoric movement is to make economists more aware of the ways in which they attempt to persuade one another regarding knowledge claims about economic phenomena. In 1990 he spoke at the plenary session of the joint meeting of the American Agricultural Economics Association and the Canadian Agricultural Economics and Farm Management Society in Vancouver (McCloskey, 1990). Several volumes of conference and symposium papers exploring a rhetorical approach to economic methodology have been published (for example Klamer *et al.*, 1988).

McCloskey has called for a fundamental re-orientation in the way that economists think about the process of theory appraisal. He rejects methodology as a normative inquiry and has encouraged economists to follow the example of literary criticism. Good economics is good conversation. The word rhetoric is often used with pejorative connotations, to signify lack of substance. In McCloskey's writings, rhetoric is used in its more traditional meaning of the study of the means of argumentation and persuasion. Rhetoric examines the ways that we accomplish things with language; how we explain, motivate and convince. It is the art of probing what economists believe and why they believe it. It examines why economists find certain types of statements convincing and not others. McCloskey maintains that a rhetorical examination of their discipline would make economists better teachers and improve the temperament of the profession.

Like Hollis and Nell, McCloskey summarizes the tenets of methodological orthodoxy in a ten item list. He calls this list the ten commandments of modernism (see Table 8.1). Like the Hollis and Nell list, these ten items represent a combination of ideas from logical positivism, Popperian falsificationism and instrumentalism. The first item on McCloskey's list is from Friedman's version of instrumentalism. Theory appraisal is based on usefulness and usefulness depends on predictive success. Items 2, 3, 5,

Table 8.1 McCloskey's 10 commandments of modernism

---

1. Prediction and control is the point of science.

2. Only the observable implications of a theory matter to its truth.

3. Observability involves objective, replicable experiments – questionnaires do not qualify.

4. If and only if experimental falsification of a theory is obtained is a theory proved false.

5. Objectivity is valuable, scientifically, introspection is not.

6. Quantification is necessary.

7. Introspection is an aid to hypothesis development but not validation.

8. Methodology separates scientific from non-scientific discourse.

9. Scientific explanation is showing that a particular instance is an example of a general 'law'.

10. Scientists should have nothing to say (as scientists) about judgements of value.

Source: McCloskey (1985, pp. 7–8).

possibly 6, 7 and 10 are derived from logical positivism. Karl Popper appears in items 4 and 8.

Modernism also views the mathematical treatment of economic theory with favour. McCloskey is less sanguine than the mainstream on this issue. Initially , mathematics seems to have helped economists sort out some of their theoretical ideas, but the cost has been a widening gulf between mathematically inclined economists and almost everyone else. Mathematics has become its own rhetoric. It has narrowed the scope of economic analysis, by advancing the creed 'If it can't be expressed as a constrained optimization problem, it isn't economics'. If the mathematical treatment of economic concepts contributed to the understanding of those concepts initially, McCloskey wonders if the process has not proceeded too far. All too often it appears that mathematical virtuosity is being pursued for its own sake, without regard for the purposes that economists have laid down for their subject.

McCloskey rejects what he calls modernism on four grounds. First, he equates modernism with logical positivism and then accuses economists as one of the few groups that have not read the philosophical obituary of that doctrine. McCloskey claims that even Karl Popper has abandoned falsification in favour of criticism. Economists have not kept up with the philosophical literature and as a result they are trying to live by a set of methodological rules that are out of date.

The second count in McCloskey's indictment of modernism is that economists do not abide by the rules of falsification. While there may be agreement in principle to the orthodox methodological view, economists have been most inventive in finding rationales for instances of falsification that have occurred. The third criticism of modernism is that its primary goal, prediction, is impossible in economics. McCloskey appeals to Ludwig von Mises's argument that economic prediction is beyond the cognitive capacity of mere mortal human beings. Mises's writings emphasized the adaptive and open-ended nature of human action. People can adjust their actions to changes in their environment, including changes in the knowledge of the environment produced by economists. This adaptation makes quantitative prediction of events impossible. McCloskey also appeals to one of the folk theorems of economics, 'If you are so smart, why aren't you rich?' If economists possessed the ability to predict future economic events, then they could act on the basis of those predictions and acquire great wealth. Few economists have acquired great wealth, therefore the predictive power of economics must be limited.

McCloskey's fourth and final argument against modernism is that it is impossible. No one abides by its precepts, but no one could abide by them. In fact, strict adherence to modernism would arrest all progress in economic research. Modernism cannot deliver on its promise of certainty in knowledge. Perhaps scientific knowledge has more in common with other branches of knowledge than modernism admits. Following Coase (1982), McCloskey argues that several events in the history of economic ideas in the twentieth century, the Keynesian revolution and the monetarist counter-revolution were flagrant violations of modernism. Many economists were persuaded of the merits of the first wave of ideas, and later of the second, long before any facts had been systematically collected or analysed.

THE FOUR KEY METHODOLOGICAL QUESTIONS

What is the Purpose of Economic Analysis?

According to McCloskey, economics is a historical, not a predictive science. The aim of economics is social self-understanding. He rejects the modernist proposition that the purpose of economic analysis is prediction and control.

He has determined that this is an impossible goal, and in a sense ends up advocating the purpose of understanding by default. McCloskey does not actually provide any reasons for this position.

Economists have been led astray by the search for a normative methodology for their discipline. McCloskey argues, passionately at times, that Paul Feyerabend has demolished the philosophy of science as the pursuit of universal rules for theory appraisal. Instead of aspiring to the traditional normative standards of methodology, economists should emphasize the study of positive methodology. They should document how economists *do* choose among competing theories, not how they *should* choose. Study of the rhetoric of economics is essential to this task. It promotes the art of discerning what economists believe and why they believe it. It examines why economists find some types of statements convincing and others not. McCloskey also suggests that the study of rhetoric would improve the ability of economists to communicate, both with others and among themselves.

In McCloskey's hands, rhetoric becomes a yardstick for 'good conversation'. Good conversation is the goal of economic inquiry. Goodness is not easy to define objectively, it is recognized intuitively. We know it when we see, or rather hear it.

What is the Source of Economic Knowledge?

If McCloskey is correct, and Feyerabend has applied the death blow to the hope of a normative methodology for science and rhetoric is the best available alternative to the practitioner of science, then this classical methodological question becomes largely irrelevant. The matter of admissibility of sources is clearly a normative question. It attempts to rule out certain sources of knowledge. A large-scale effort in rhetorical economics would presumably treat the writings of economists as the primary source of economic knowledge, or at least of knowledge about the rhetoric of economics. McCloskey outlines this approach in Chapters 5 to 9 of his book. He applies rhetorical analysis to selected passages from the writings of Paul Samuelson, Gary Becker, Robert Solow, Richard Muth and Robert Fogel. The results of this analysis are revealing, in terms of the way that these influential economists structure their presentations. McCloskey selects two pages at random from Samuelson's *Foundations*. In those pages, he detects what he describes as an 'Easy air of mathematical mastery'. This gives an impression of virtuosity that McCloskey likens to the use of Latin and Greek by nineteenth century British writers. The impression intimidates, through expressions such as 'The demonstration of this result is left as an exercise for the interested reader'. McCloskey identifies six appeals to authority, several appeals to the virtue of 'relaxing assumptions', additional appeals to the properties of a hypothetical economy, with suggestions that these correspond to actual properties of some real economy and one use of metaphor.

McCloskey's examples of rhetorical textual analysis of economists' writings are illuminating and provocative. We are not used to seeing ourselves from this perspective. What we see is often not flattering, in that it does not appear to live up to the standard of the objective impartial pursuit of knowledge.

What is the Scope of Economic Analysis?

This question is also normative, and therefore of little interest to a rhetoritician of economics. 'Economics is what economists do' is a satisfactory definition of the scope of the discipline for the purposes of rhetorical analysis. Like Bruce Caldwell, McCloskey calls for pluralism in the methodology of economics. He describes this as anarchy: 'Let the only rule be that there are no other rules'. But McCloskey's anarchy implicitly invokes other rules. Is any method of persuasion really acceptable to an anarchist? What about fraudulent persuasion? What about force? I suspect that McCloskey really wants to describe himself as a methodological libertarian. Consent is the test of acceptable persuasion.

What is the Appropriate Structure of a Scientific Theory?

Once again, this normative question is out of order. It is presumptuous to presume the existence of a correct structure for economic theory. Economists should rather seek good conversation. McCloskey is not so much concerned with the structure of theory as with the structure of relationships and communication in the community of scholars. This community extends beyond the boundaries of practitioners of the discipline of economics. An economics that is unaware of its own rhetoric can remain isolated within this broader community, and, in fact, this has largely been the case (McCloskey, 1988, p. 286). Economics has largely ignored its critics from without.

ASSESSING THE RHETORICAL APPROACH TO ECONOMIC METHODOLOGY

An awareness of rhetoric may indeed improve the conversation of economics. It may make economists more aware of the literature and the history of the development of ideas of their subject. It may make them better communicators, both among themselves and in their interactions with non-economists. Economics has developed a distinctive culture (Leijonhufvud, 1973), and it has developed a cultural rhetoric. Economists use literary devices including metaphors and analogies. McCloskey's rhetorical analysis of selections from Samuelson's *Foundations* points out several appeals to the properties of a hypothetical economy.[1] These properties are implicitly attributed to an actual economy, although the basis for this correspondence is not provided. Economists also appeal to authority, introspection, economic intuition and other aspects of the faculty of reason in ways not officially permitted under modernism.

The use of mathematics by economists, as Richard Levins (1989, 1992) has so poignantly demonstrated, may obscure as much of the logical structure of economic theory as it elucidates. If the rhetorical analysis of economics does nothing more than cause economists to be more aware of the implicit presuppositions of their own writing, it will have accomplished a great deal.

Like Caldwell, McCloskey advocates pluralism in the methodology of economics.[2] Pluralism has much to recommend it if it contributes to tolerance and broadens the scope of inquiry in a discipline. Whether such breadth is desirable in economic scholarship at the present time depends on one's answer to the question posed in the first chapter of this book. Is there a crisis in economic theory? An answer in the affirmative would support the case for breadth. Widening the scope of inquiry might lead to discoveries that could resolve the crisis. If there is no crisis, breadth is dissipating.

A RHETORICAL ANALYSIS OF 'THE RHETORIC OF ECONOMICS'

Although McCloskey encourages economists to be more conscious of their rhetoric, in some respects, he frequently fails to take his own advice. Although he is critical of economists' dependence on appeal to authority in their writing, many of his arguments are based on just such appeals. Feyerabend, in particular, is quoted as an argument clincher on numerous occasions. McCloskey is not always careful about the definitions of the terms that he uses. He describes himself as a realist and as an anarchist, although it is far from clear that he holds either of these views. Realism (see Chapter 7) is a normative methodological doctrine. It has a great deal to say about the appropriate structure of a scientific theory and about the normative evaluation of theories. All this is anathema to McCloskey's interpretation of Feyerabend. His description of modernism also fails to distinguish between logical positivism and instrumentalism and Popper's falsificationism.

Perhaps McCloskey simply makes too much of rhetoric. It is one thing to say that greater awareness of the ideas of literary criticism and more sensitivity on the part of economists to the rhetorical, literary and mathematical devices that they use in their efforts to inform and persuade one another would have a beneficial impact on disciplinary conversation. It is quite another to suggest that rhetoric can provide a comprehensive framework for theory assessment or for the validation of knowledge claims of economists. It is much easier to accept the first of these propositions than the second.

QUESTIONS FOR DISCUSSION

1.   Find some examples of rhetorical devices that economists use in their conversations with one another.
2.   Can rhetorical analysis replace normative methodology in economics?
3.   Compare and contrast McCloskey's ten Commandments of modernism (Table 8.1) with Hollis and Nell's ten tenets of neoclassical economics (Table 6.1).

NOTES

1.   Lucas (1980) formalized this use of analogy in relating models of hypothetical economies to an actual economy.
2.   He does not seem to see the irony in, on the one hand rejecting the notion of a normative economic methodology, and then proceeding to recommend a norm, 'Let a thousand flowers bloom'.

9. Is Economics a Science?

A PERSONAL DIGRESSION

I took a course in plant physiology when I was an undergraduate student. The course was organized around the question 'How does water move up the stems of plants?'. It is not hard to determine that water does make its way from the roots of plants to the uppermost leaves and stems, and it is natural enough for the scientifically inquisitive to want to know how. We began with what was to be a series of theories offering explanations. The first lecture examined Theory 1. For the benefit of the sceptics in the class, this was followed by a laboratory demonstration. This demonstrated that movement of water up the stem of the plants used in that lab was consistent with the model presented in the lecture.

In the next lecture, however, the instructor explained that the previous week's theory could only account for the movement of water in plants up to about one foot in height. He then proceeded to present Theory 2. This was followed by a lab demonstration. But the following week he told us that this new theory could only account for movement of water up the stems of plants about 1 metre in height. This pattern was repeated each week of the semester.

In the last lecture of the course, the professor admitted that plant physiologists still did not have a satisfactory explanation of how the tallest trees managed to transport water to their uppermost branches. I was deeply impressed. This course changed my impression of what science was all about. Rather than being the path to certain knowledge following the clearly illuminated steps of logic, I began to see it as an open-ended and only occasionally successful instrument for the apprehension of truth.

A RECAPITULATION

The preceding eight chapters of this book have been devoted to violating George Stigler's dictum that economists should be forbidden from studying methodology until they are at least 65 years of age. Like James Buchanan, I believe that knowledge of methodology at least prepares the research economist to ask promising questions. If the study of methodology is undertaken in order to determine if a particular field of scholarship is a science, however, then methodologists of economics have much work to do.

As we saw in the first chapter, criticism from within seems to be growing in economics. Doubts about the empirical foundations of the discipline, about the growth of formalism, about the basis for economists' claims of knowledge about human social interaction and about the relationship between economic theories and actual economic phenomena are being raised with increasing frequency in high places. As we saw in the second chapter, economists agree on more ideas than they are generally given credit for, but the basis for this agreement, and by implication the reasons for disagreement when that occurs, are far from clear.

This book provides an introduction to the methodologies of economics. The use of the plural is deliberate. There are several methodologies for economics. Philosophically, economics is a house divided. Most economists who have written on methodology have combined elements from various methodological doctrines in an eclectic manner. But these hybrid methodologies are not coherent. Methodological discussion among economists is made more difficult by the variations in meaning attached to certain fundamental terms. For example theory, model, assumption, prediction, explanation and rationality are all used in a variety of ways in professional discourse. Economists do not agree on the fundamental purpose of their subject. As a result, they cannot agree on the basis for specific claims of knowledge. Methodology is concerned with theory appraisal. It seeks a protocol for the criticism of knowledge claims about the phenomena investigated by a particular discipline. It is a theory of theories. The most basic methodological question concerns the purpose of inquiry in a discipline. Economists are generally split on whether the purpose of economic investigation should be to understand or to explain economic phenomena. Many economists invoke both goals as synonymous, but as I argued earlier, there are important distinctions between the two. Understanding involves acquiring the perspective of the insider, able to apprehend the meaning and the purpose behind people's actions. Explanation is less ambitious. Explanation seeks to show that a particular phenomenon is an example of a more general law or principle. It stops short of seeking the meaning or purpose of that general law. Most economists subscribe to some version of logical positivism and Popperian falsificationism as described by Mark Blaug. But this comfortable consensus is undermined by the growing chorus of voices rejecting logical positivism as an incoherent doctrine of scientific method. The Karl Popper of 1935, and this is the Karl Popper that economists have sought to appease, is not the Karl Popper of 1963. Critical rationalism has not been enthusiastically embraced by the discipline. Most economists, and Donald McCloskey is a noteworthy exception, do not wish to see literary criticism as the role model for their research.

Milton Friedman's controversial instrumentalism is also problematic. Alexander Rosenberg and Daniel Hausman have constructed a compelling case that the prospects for a predictively successful economic science are not good. The track record of economics since the publication of Friedman's essay is not comforting either. The list of events that economists have failed to anticipate is a long one. Our record of being able to agree on just what predictions follow from economic theory is not very impressive either.

The minority doctrines of economic methodology, *a priorism*, scientific realism, rhetoric and textual criticism, all suffer from marginalization. Few economists are aware of the ideas that make up these points of view, and it is difficult to sustain a substantive disciplinary conversation on any one of them.[1] This is not to say that these alternative paradigms are not of value. In my judgement, they have much to say that is of value. But it is difficult for this value to be appreciated unless a more tolerant view of the nature of scientific economics is established.

The upshot of this brief synopsis of earlier chapters is that current methodological orthodoxy is precarious. Economists believe many things about the nature of science and the cognitive status of their discipline that have been rejected by philosophers of science. Many of the things that economists believe about science are an eclectic and inconsistent mixture of ideas from competing philosophies of science. Phelby (1988) contends that economists have been overly influenced by the methodological orthodoxy of natural science in a bygone era. Several methodologists are now questioning if the idealized world of that bygone era ever really existed. Methodological complacency among economists would therefore seem to be misplaced.

RECENT DEVELOPMENTS IN THE PHILOSOPHY OF ECONOMICS

Daniel Hausman begins his recent book, *The Inexact and Separate Science of Economics* (1992), with an affirmation of methodological ideas that could have been lifted from the pages of Lionel Robbins's essay. Economic science is deductive. It uses logic to derive the consequences of a few basic axioms. The confidence that economists place on their theories derives from their confidence in those axioms, and not in the empirical testing of the implications of those axioms. This, according to Hausman's interpretation, is the traditional view on the methodology of economics. It has been abandoned, he estimates, for two generations, when it was wrongly snubbed by the economist followers of logical positivism.

Economists' knowledge of causal relationships comes from introspection, as in the case of actions being motivated by self-interest, or from technical knowledge from other fields, interpreted from an economic perspective, such as the law of diminishing returns. But these causal relationships, according to Hausman, are 'tendencies'. In any given situation, there are many variables that can interfere with these causal relationships. These variables are not encompassed by economic theory, and make the operation of economic causal relationships inexact.   Hausman takes a post-positivist, post-Popperian position.   In fact, he calls for a return to the methodological position that prevailed in economics prior to the 1930s.   He draws extensively on the ideas of J.S. Mill, on *a priorism* or deductivism.   He argues that this methodological position has been what economists actually practice, contrary to the officially orthodox positivism of the last 60 years, and that this closet methodology is satisfactory for economics.   The particular focus of his inquiry is neoclassical microeconomics, which Hausman characterizes as the theories of consumer choice and the theory of the firm interacting under conditions of pervasive and perpetual equilibrium.   Consumers act so as to maximize utility, with complete, transitive and continuous preferences.   Firms maximize profits, while operating under diminishing returns to the application of any particular factor and with constant returns to scale with respect to all factors.   Pervasive and perpetual equilibrium in the markets for factors of production and for products implies that the theory is suspicious of claims of persistent opportunities to exploit resource owners, households or firms.   The mystery that intrigues Hausman is the often apparently dogmatic allegiance of economists to this framework in the face of troubling empirical anomalies that seem to indicate that it is descriptively false in its characterization of human behaviour.   Why do economists continue to employ this paradigm when they generally reject the validity of most of its constituent elements as a representation of economic phenomena?

According to Hausman, much that has been written on economic methodology is misguided because it has failed to appreciate the importance of neoclassical microeconomics as a template that outlines that strategy and structure of economic inquiry.   Most mainstream economists are not committed to the validity of all of the elements of neoclassical microeconomics, they are committed to not abandoning all of the elements at once.   The paradigm uses the theory as a reference point to explore the consequences of abandoning these elements one at time.   The justification for continued allegiance to neoclassical microeconomics derives from the poor quality of economic data.   Empirical anomalies that appear to contradict elements of the theory may be indicative of the inadequacy of the theory, or they may be a statistical mirage.   Given the level of doubt regarding the validity and accuracy of economic observations themselves, so the argument goes, it is better to doubt the data than the theory, at least until a more or less fully articulated alternative theory comes along.   This is what Hausman calls the 'weak-link' principle.   If a false conclusion depends on several premises, each of which is not known to be true, doubt the premise that is most uncertain.

Like Hollis and Nell, Caldwell, McCloskey, Rothbard and Mises, Hausman sees the era of the influence of positivism in economics as a dead end.   His recommendation is a return to a rehabilitated *a priorism*.   Unfortunately, he does not discuss the ideas of the twentieth century *a priorists* in sufficient detail to indicate whether he agrees with post-Mill *a priorists*. Like Leontief, Hausman calls for increased emphasis on improving the quality and the quantity of economic data. This includes a more 'open minded' attitude towards data sources such as surveys and experiments. He also encourages economists to interact more with other social scientists, and in fact to use their data in economic research, and to be more tolerant of different styles of theorizing, such as those employed in business schools and by institutional economists.

IN PURSUIT OF SCIENTIFIC ECONOMICS

How might we determine if economics is a science? If an accepted universal statement of the nature of scientific inquiry were available, we could compare the state of economics to the general standards for science. Either economics would pass muster or it would not. A generation ago, methodologists were comfortable making these types of assessments. The criteria for 'Scienceness' were clear. The only issue was whether or not economics fit the mould. But the philosophy of science is not what it used to be. We are much less sure of what it means to be scientific.

We could follow George Stigler's (1983) community model of science. In his Nobel lecture, Stigler attributes three characteristics to a science. First, it has produced an 'integrated body of knowledge'. Second, the extension and development of this knowledge is undertaken by a group of interacting practitioners. These practitioners devoted a large part of their lives to the validation and extension of this knowledge. Cumulative improvement in the knowledge produced by this community is the third hallmark of science. Clearly, economics meets this standard, at least on the first two criteria. But so do astrology, theology and musicology. The community model is too inclusive. Too many human intellectual pursuits qualify as science under this definition.

The third of Stigler's characteristics is difficult to assess without objective standards of what constitutes improvement. Ronald Coase, one of Stigler's University of Chicago colleagues, does not give late twentieth century economics a passing grade on cumulative progress.

Later in Stigler's Nobel lecture, he refocuses the purpose of economics: 'The central task of an empirical science such as economics is to provide general understanding of events in the real world, and ultimately all of its theories and techniques must be instrumental to that task' (p. 533). This gives us some indication of what cumulative progress might involve. An empirical science requires a set of durable and fundamental problems in order to allow scientists to master their subject matter and validate their findings. This is what Maurice Allais (1989) has described as the need for 'the existence of regularities that can be analyzed and forecast'. In fact, Allais argues that economic phenomena exhibit this such regularity and therefore economics is a science.

A second approach would be to more thoroughly and consciously investigate the various methodological views that have been articulated by economists from time to time. A more tolerant and rigorous conversation that respects the ideals of McCloskey's anarchy or Caldwell's pluralism has much to recommend it. At the very least, this consciousness-raising exercise would reveal the extensive and arbitrary methodological eclecticism that all too often passes for philosophy in the discipline.

A more difficult and less travelled road would involve economists in the definition of what constitutes scientific economics. Rather that wait for illumination about the true nature of science from without, economists could construct their own standard. This process is actually under way, although the final outlines of what it will produce are far from clear.

Let me offer some preliminary impressions. First, economist–philosophers and philosopher–economists seem to be converging on the idea that economics in particular and the social sciences in general are different from the natural sciences. This is a difference in kind and not just in degree. Investigation in the social sciences confronts the meaning of phenomena, in addition to their explanation. The distinction between understanding and explanation is critical in the social sciences. It is meaningless in the natural sciences. Chemists do not aspire, as chemists at least, to apprehend the meaning of the periodic table. The properties of the elements are what they are. Elements do not choose. They do not act, they re-act. Social scientists have access to insider knowledge about what it means to prefer, to choose and to act that has no counterpart in the natural sciences.

Second, it is becoming more widely accepted that the nature of prediction is different in the natural sciences than it is in economics. Economic theory sees people as learning, choosing beings. Choosing and acting are conditioned on experience or environment, but only a few materialist determinists would argue that choice is entirely circumscribed by objective external conditions. Human behaviour is adaptive in a more proactive way than a stimulus response relationship admits. Human action is animated by preferences, expectations and perceptions. All of these are subjective, and therefore at best incompletely accessible to external observers. Without the ability to objectively measure the state of subjective states of mind, economists know that their models will always be missing important variables and relationships. We should only expect limited predictive success.

It is becoming commonplace for economists to describe their discipline as an 'inexact science'. It is not yet clear that this description means the same thing each time that it is used. In some contexts, it seems to refer to the problem of the number of significant digits in economic data. Elsewhere, it refers to the problem of the reliability of the sources of data. Inexactness can also be used to describe the transitory nature of estimates of parameters in econometric models as technology, tastes and policies change.

THE CONTRIBUTIONS OF METHODOLOGY

The study of methodology offers several contributions to economic discourse. First, the study of methodology cultivates awareness of the diversity of perspectives held by economists. This diversity extends to ideas about the purpose and even the definition of the subject. It is difficult to apprehend from casual reading of introductory chapters of textbooks, where methodological propositions are most frequently articulated. At first blush, most of these chapters seem to be saying the same thing. Closer methodological investigation reveals subtle but important differences. These differences contribute to different perceptions of economic problems and to differences in research priorities.

A second contribution of methodology is a greater awareness of what we might call foundations. How do economists know what they know? What is the relationship between theory and phenomena? What are legitimate sources of knowledge in the validation of theory? What is the nature of the relationship between the properties of a hypothetical economy in which all agents are constrained optimizers with rational expectations and in which all markets clear all of the time and the economy of any particular human society? What is the basis for agreement and disagreement among economists on these questions? Foundations also involve the clarification of core ideas. What do economists mean by predictions? What is the nature of cause and effect in economic theory? What is the difference between a model and a theory? The examination of foundations compels us to take the rhetoric of our subject more seriously. It requires that we be more conscious of the ways in which we attempt to persuade ourselves and others about the validity of our claims of knowledge about the world in which we live.

Third, methodology makes us more conscious of the nature of criticism in our discipline. Popper has argued that a tradition for giving and receiving criticism is the most important source of knowledge that any discipline possesses. The study of methodology makes the maintenance of this tradition deliberate and overt.

Since about 1970, methodology has become an increasingly active area of research in economics. The initial motivation for this work, as exemplified by Bell and Kristol's *The Crisis in Economic Theory* (eds, 1981), was the disintegration of macroeconomics as a coherent body of knowledge. Macroeconomists knew, or thought they knew, a lot more about their subject in 1967 than they know in 1997. It should not be surprising that economists have taken to asking themselves increasingly fundamental philosophical questions.

Methodology has still not achieved the status or the influence of a core field in economics. Perhaps we wish that the questions that methodologists ask would just go away. But it is difficult for me to see how this could happen. As for the view that methodology should be pursued only as a descriptive and not as a prescriptive research programme, this fails to offer a satisfying alternative. To abandon methodology as a normative inquiry denies the need for theory appraisal and criticism. It surrenders the battle to separate valid knowledge claims from the musings of eccentrics. The fact that the methodology of economics has not yet produced generally accepted criteria for theory appraisal is no reason to give up the chase.

QUESTIONS FOR DISCUSSION

1.   Should economists evaluate their theories by the same standards as those used by their counterparts in the natural sciences?
2.   Is it worth the trouble for economists to study methodology?
3.   Is economics a science?
4.   What are the strengths and weaknesses of the five methodological schools that have been examined in this book?

NOTE

1.   Isolated enclaves talk among themselves in methodological ghettos, but relations with outsiders rarely go deeper than reciprocal name-calling.

References

Allais, M. (1989), 'The Economic Science of Today and Facts: A Critical Analysis of Some Characteristic Features', Lecture given at the University of Ottawa, 23 May.

Alston, R., J.R. Kearl and M.B. Vaughan (1992), 'Is There a Consensus Among Economists in the 1990s', *American Economic Review*, 82(2):203–9.

American Economic Review (1993), 'Petition to Reform Graduate Education', *American Economic Review*, December.

Appelbaum, E. (1978), 'Testing Neoclassical Production Theory', *Journal of Econometrics*, 7(1):87–102.

Arrow, K. (1951), *Social Choice and Individual Values*, Yale University Press, New Haven.

Becker, G. (1976), *The Economic Approach to Human Behaviour*, ago Press, Chicago.

Bell, D. and I. Kristol (eds) (1981), *The Crisis in Economic Theory*, Basic Books, New York.

Bhaskar, R. (1975), *A Realist Theory of Science*, Leeds Books, Leeds.

Black, F. (1982), 'The Trouble with Econometric Models', *Financial Analysts Journal*, 35(March/April): 3–11.

Blaug, M. (1980), *The Methodology of Economics or How Economists Explain*, Cambridge University Press, Cambridge.

Blaug, M. (1992), *The Methodology of Economics or How Economists Explain* (2nd Edition), Cambridge University Press, Cambridge.

Block, W. (1986), *The US Bishops and Their Critics*, Fraser Institute, Vancouver.

Block, W. and M. Walker (1988), 'Entropy in the Canadian Economics Profession', *Canadian Public Policy*, 14(June):137–50.

Boland, L. (1979), 'A Critique of Friedman's Critics' *Journal of Economic Literature*, 17(June):503–22.

Boland, L. (1981), 'On the Futility of Criticizing the Neoclassical Maximization Hypothesis', *American Economic Review*, 71(1):71–80.

Boland, L. (1982), *The Foundations of Economic Method*, George Allen & Unwin, London.

Boland, L. (1989), *The Methodology of Economic Model Building: Methodology After Samuelson*, Routledge, London.

Boyd, R. (1983), 'On the Current Status of Scientific Realism', *Erkenntnis*, 19:45–90.

Buchanan, J.M. (1964), 'What Should Economists Do?', *Southern Economic Journal*, 30(3):213–22.

Buchanan, J.M. (1979), *What Should Economists Do?*, Liberty Press, Indianapolis.

Buchanan, J. and G. Tullock (1962), *The Calculus of Consent*, University of Michigan Press, Ann Arbor.

Cairnes, J.E. (1888/1965), *Character and Logical Method of Political Economy* (2nd Edition), A.M. Kelley, New York.

Caldwell, B. (1982), *Beyond Positivism: Economic Methodology in the Twentieth Century*, Unwin Hyman, London.

Caldwell, B. (ed.) (1984a), *Appraisal and Criticism in Economics: A Book of Readings*, Allen & Unwin, Boston.

Caldwell, B. (1984b), 'Praxeology and Its Critics', *History of Political Economy*, 16(3):363–79.

Caldwell, B. (1990), 'Does Methodology Matter? How Should it be Practiced?', *Finnish Economic Papers*, 3(1):64–71.

Caldwell, B. (1991), 'Clarifying Popper', *Journal of Economic Literature*, 29(1):1–33.

Cheung, S. (1978), *The Myth of Social Cost*, Institute of Economic Affairs, London.

Cheung, S. (1983), 'The Contractual Nature of the Firm', *Journal of Law and Economics,* 26:1–21

Coase, R. (1937/1988), 'The Nature of the Firm', *Economica*, 4:386–406. Reprinted in *The Firm, the Market and the Law*.

Coase, R. (1939), 'Rowland Hill and the Penny Post', *Economica*, 6:423–35.

Coase, R. (1946/1988), 'The Marginal Cost Controversy', *Economica*, 13:169–82. Reprinted in *The Firm, the Market and the Law*.

Coase, R. (1950), *British Broadcasting: A Study in Monopoly*, Longmans Green & Co., London.

Coase, R. (1959), 'The Federal Communications Commission', *Journal of Law and Economics*, 2:1–40.

Coase, R. (1960/1988), 'The Problem of Social Cost', *Journal of Law and Economics*, 3:1–44. Reprinted in *The Firm, the Market and the Law*.

Coase, R. (1962), 'The Interdependent Radio Advisory Committee', *Journal of Law and Economics*, 5:17–47.

Coase, R. (1970), 'The Theory of Public Utility Pricing and Its Application', *Bell Journal of Economics and Management Science,* 1:113–28.

Coase, R. (1972), 'Durability and Monopoly', *Journal of Law and Economics*, 15:143–9.

Coase, R. (1974), 'The Market for Goods and the Market for Ideas', *American Economic Review*, 64:384–91.

Coase, R. (1974/1988), 'The Lighthouse in Economics', *Journal of Law and Economics*, **17**:357–76. Reprinted in *The Firm, the Market and the Law.*

Coase, R. (1975), 'Marshall on Method', *Journal of Law and Economics*, **18**(1):25–32.

Coase, R. (1977), 'Advertising and Free Speech', *Journal of Legal Studies*, **6**:1–34.

Coase, R. (1981), 'The Coase Theorem and the Empty Core: A Comment', *Journal of Law and Economics*, **24**:183–7.

Coase, R. (1982), 'How Should Economists Choose?', G. Warren Nutter Lecture in Political Economy, American Enterprise Institute, Washington, DC.

Coase, R. (1988a), *The Firm, the Market and the Law*, University of Chicago Press, Chicago.

Coase, R. (1988b), 'Notes on the Problem of Social Cost', in *The Firm, the Market and the Law*, University of Chicago Press, Chicago.

Coase, R. and R. Fowler (1935a), 'Bacon Production and the Pig Cycle in Great Britain', *Economica,* May:142–67.

Coase, R. and R. Fowler (1935b), 'The Pig-Cycle: A Rejoinder', *Economica,* November:423–8.

Coase, R. and R. Fowler (1937), 'The Pig-Cycle in Great Britain: An Explanation', *Economica*, February:55–82.

Coase, R. and R. Fowler (1940), 'The Analysis of Producers' Expectations', *Economica*, August:280–92.

Colander, D. and R. Brenner (eds) (1992), *Educating Economists*, University of Michigan Press, Ann Arbor.

Colander, D. and A. Klamer (1987), 'The Making of an Economist', *Journal of Economic Perspectives,* **1**(2):95–111.

Coleman, J. (1992), *Risks and Wrongs*, Cambridge Studies in Philosophy and Law, Cambridge University Press, Cambridge.

Cordato, R. (1992), *Welfare Economics and Externalities in an Open Ended Universe*, Kluwer, Boston.

Cozzarin, B. and B. Gilmour (forthcoming), 'A Methodological Evaluation of Empirical Demand Systems Research', *Canadian Journal of Agricultural Economics.*

de Marchi, N. (ed.) (1988), *The Popperian Legacy in Economics*, Cambridge University Press, Cambridge.

Debreu, G. (1959), *Theory of Value*, Wiley, New York.

Debreu, G. (1984), 'Economic Theory in the Mathematical Mode', *American Economic Review*, **74**(3):267–78.

Debreu, G. (1991), 'The Mathematization of Economic Theory', *American Economic Review*, **81**(1):1–7.

Dewald, W., J. Thursby and R. Anderson (1986), 'Replication in Empirical Economics: The *Journal of Money, Credit and Banking* Project', *American Economic Review*, **76**(4):587–603.

Dingle, M. (1980), 'The Historical Significance of Today's Economics', *History of Economics Society Bulletin*, 2:18–9.

Eichner, A. (1983), 'Why Economics is Not Yet a Science', *Journal of Economic Issues*, 27(2):507–20.

Evans, D. (1928), *New Realism and Old Reality: A Critical Introduction to the Philosophy of the New Realists*, Princeton University Press, Princeton, NJ.

Feyerabend, P. (1981), *Realism, Rationalism and Scientific Method* (Philosophical papers Vol. 1), Cambridge University Press, Cambridge.

Fox, G. (1988), Review of *Long Waves of Regional Development* by M. Marshall, *American Journal of Agricultural Economics*, 70(2):494–5.

Fox, G. and L. Kivanda (1994), 'Popper or Production', *Canadian Journal of Agricultural Economics*, 42(1):1–14.

Frey, B. and R. Eichenberger (1992), 'Economics and Economists: A European Perspective', *American Economic Review*, 82(2):216–20.

Frey, B., W. Pommerehne, F. Schneider and G. Gilbert (1984), 'Consensus and Dissension Among Economists', *American Economic Review*, 74(5):986–94.

Friedman, M. (1953), *Essays in Positive Economics*, University of Chicago Press, Chicago.

Gauthier, D. (1985), *Morals by Agreement*, Clarendon Press, Oxford.

Gerrard, B. (1990), 'On Matters Methodological in Economics', *Journal of Economic Surveys*, 4(2):197–219.

Goodhart, C. (1978), 'Problems of Monetary Management: the U.K. Experience' in A. Lourakis (ed.), *Inflation, Depression and Economic Policy in the West*, Basil Blackwell, Oxford.

Hansen, W. (1991), 'The Education and Training of Economics Doctorates: Major Findings of the American Economic Association's Commission on Graduate Education in Economics', *Journal of Economic Literature*, 29(3):1054–87.

Hausman, D. (ed.) (1984), *The Philosophy of Economics: An Anthology*, Cambridge University Press, Cambridge.

Hausman, D. (1988), 'An Appraisal of Popperian Methodology', in N. De Marchi (ed.), *The Popperian Legacy in Economics*, Cambridge University Press, Cambridge.

Hausman, D. (1992), *The Inexact and Separate Science of Economics*, Cambridge University Press, Cambridge.

Hausman, D. and M. McPherson (undated), 'Agricultural Economics and the Chaos of Economic Methodology', *Journal of Agricultural Economics Research*, 42(2):3–4.

Hayek, F. (1944/1991), 'On Being an Economist', in W.W. Bartley III and S. Kresge (eds), *The Trend of Economic Thinking*, University of Chicago Press, Chicago, pp. 35–48.

Hayek, F. (1948), *Individualism and Economic Order*, University of Chicago Press, Chicago.

Hayek, F. (1964), *The Counter-Revolution of Science*, Free Press of Glencoe, Glencoe.

Hayek, F. (1973/1976/1979), *Law, Legislation and Liberty* (Vols 1, 2 and 3), University of Chicago Press, Chicago.

Hayek, F. (1978), *New Studies in Philosophy, Politics, Economics and the History of Ideas*, University of Chicago Press, Chicago.

Hayek, F. (1988), *The Fatal Conceit: The Errors of Socialism*, University of Chicago Press, Chicago.

Hamouda, O.F. and B.B. Price (1991), *Verification in Economics and History*, Routledge, London.

Hazlitt, H. (1946/1979), *Economics in One Lesson*, Harper, New York (1946) and Arlington House (1979).

Heilbroner, R. (1980), 'Modern Economics as a Chapter in the History of Economic Thought', *Challenge,* January/February:20–24.

Henderson, J. and R. Quandt (1980), *Microeconomic Theory.* McGraw-Hill, New York.

Hendry, D. (1980), 'Econometrics–Alchemy or Science?' *Economica*, November:387–406.

Hollis, M. (1994), *The Philosophy of Social Science*, Cambridge University Press, Cambridge.

Hollis, M. and E. Nell (1975), *Rational Economic Man*, Cambridge University Press, Cambridge.

Hooker, C. (1987), *A Realistic Theory of Science*, State University of New York Press, Albany.

Hoppe, H.H. (1988), *Praxeology and Economic Science*, Ludwig von Mises Institute, Auburn.

Hutchison, T. (1938), *The Significance and Basic Postulates of Economic Theory*, Kelley, New York.

Hutchison, T. (1978), *On Revolutions and Progress in Economic Knowledge*, Cambridge University Press, Cambridge.

Hutchison, T. (1981), *The Politics and Philosophy of Economics*, New York University Press, New York.

Hutchison, T. (1983), *Methodological Controversy in Economics: Historical Essays in Honour of T.W. Hutchison*, JAI Press, Greenwich, Connecticut.

Hutchison, T. (1992), *Changing Aims in Economics*, Blackwell, Oxford.

Just, R. and G. Rauser (1989), 'An Assessment of the Agricultural Economics Profession', *American Journal of Agricultural Economics*, 71(5):1177–90.

Kantorovich, L. (1989), 'Mathematics in Economics: Achievements, Difficulties, Perspectives', *American Economic Review*, 79(6):18–24.

Kasper, H. *et al.* (1991), 'The Education of Economists: From Undergraduate to Graduate Study', *Journal of Economic Literature*, 29(2):1088–109.

Kearl, J., C. Pope, G. Whiting and L. Wimmer (1979), 'What Economists Think? A Confusion of Economists', *American Economic Review*, **69**(1):28–37.

Keynes, J.M. (1939), 'Professor Tinbergen's Method', *Economic Journal*, **49**:558–68.

Keynes, J.N. (1963), *The Scope and Method of Political Economy*, A.M. Kelley, New York.

Kirzner, I. (1973), *Competition and Entrepreneurship*, University of Chicago Press, Chicago.

Kirzner, I. (1985), *Discovery and the Capitalist Process*, University of Chicago Press, Chicago.

Klamer, A. and D. Colander (1990), *The Making of an Economist*, Westview Press, Boulder, Colo.

Klamer, A., D. McCloskey and R. Solow (eds) (1988), *The Consequences of Economic Rhetoric*, Cambridge University Press, Cambridge.

Klant, J. (1984), *The Rules of the Game: The Structure of Economic Theories*, Cambridge University Press, Cambridge.

Knight, F. (1921), *Risk, Uncertainty and Profit*, Houghton Mifflin, Boston.

Krueger, A. *et al.* (1991), 'Report of the Commission on Graduate Education in Economics', *Journal of Economic Literature*, **29**(3):1035–53.

Kuhn, T. (1970), *The Structure of Scientific Revolutions* (2nd Edition), University of Chicago Press, Chicago.

Kuttner, R. (1985), 'The Poverty of Economics', *Atlantic Monthly*, February:74–84.

Lachmann, L. (1986), *The Market As An Economic Process*, Basil Blackwell, New York.

Lakatos, I. (1978), *The Methodology of Scientific Research Programs*, Cambridge University Press, Cambridge.

Landes, W., D. Carlton and F. Easterbrook (1983), 'On the Resignation of Ronald H. Coase', *Journal of Law and Economics*, 26.

Latsis, S. (ed.) (1976), *Method and Appraisal in Economics*, Cambridge University Press, Cambridge.

Laudan, L. (1981), 'A Confutation of Convergent Realism', *Philosophy of Science*, **48**:19–48.

Lavoie, D. (1985), *Rivalry and Central Planning: The Socialist Calculation Debate Reconsidered*, Cambridge University Press, New York.

Lawson, T. (1989), 'Realism and Instrumentalism in the Development of Economics', *Oxford Economic Papers*, **41**(1):236–58.

Lawson, T. (1992), 'Realism, Closed Systems and Friedman', in *Research in the History of Economic Thought and Methodology*, **10**:149–9.

Leamer, E. (1983), 'Let's Take the Con Out of Econometrics', *American Economic Review*, **73**(1):31–43.

Leijonhufvud, A. (1973), 'Life Among the Econ', *Western Economic Journal*, September: 327–37.

Leontief, W. (1971), 'Theoretical Assumptions and Nonobserved Facts', *American Economic Review*, **60**(1):1–7.

Leontief, W. (1982), 'Academic Economics', Letter to the editor, *Science*, 217 (9 July): 104–7.

Lester, R. (1946), 'Shortcomings of Marginal Analysis for Wage-Employment Problems', *American Economic Review*, **36**(1):63–82.

Lester, R. (1947), 'Marginalism, Minimum Wages and Labour Markets', *American Economic Review*, **37**(1):135–48.

Levins, R. (1989), 'On Farmers Who Solve Equations', *Choices*, 4th Quarter: 8–10 (see also comments and replies in subsequent issues of *Choices*).

Levins, R. (1992), 'The Whimsical Science', *Review of Agricultural Economics*, **14**(1):139–51.

Lucas, R. (1980), 'Methods and Problems in Business Cycle Theory', *Journal of Money, Credit and Banking*, **12**(1):696–715.

Machina, M. (1987), 'Choice Under Uncertainty: Problems Solved and Unsolved', *Journal of Economic Perspectives*, **1**(1):121–54.

Machlup, F. (1978), *Methodology of Economics and the Other Social Sciences*, Academic Press, New York.

Maki, U. (1988a), 'Realism, Economics and Rhetoric', *Economics and Philosophy*, **4**:167–9.

Maki, U. (1988b), 'On the Problem of Realism in Economics', *Fundamenta Scientiae*, **9**(2/3):353–73.

Maki, U. (1988c), 'How to Combine Rhetoric and Realism in the Methodology of Economics', *Economics and Philosophy*, **4**:89–109.

Maki, U. (1989), 'On the Problem of Realism in Economics', *Richerche Economiche*, **43**(1–2):176–98.

Maki, U. (1990a), 'Scientific Realism and Austrian Explanation', *Review of Political Economy*, **2**:310–44.

Maki, U. (1990b), 'Mengerian Economics in a Realist Perspective', Karl Menger and His Legacy in Economics (annual supplement to Volume 23), *History of Political Economy*, edited by B.J. Caldwell, Duke University Press, Durham.

Marshall, M. (1987), *Long Waves of Regional Development*, St. Martin's Press, New York.

May, R. (1973), *Stability and Complexity in Model Ecosystems*, Princeton University Press, Princeton.

McCloskey, D. (1983), 'The Rhetoric of Economics', *Journal of Economic Literature*, **21**(2):481–517.

McCloskey, D. (1985), *The Rhetoric of Economics*, University of Wisconsin Press, Madison.

McCloskey, D. (1988), 'Two Replies and a Dialogue on the Rhetoric of Economics', *Economics and Philosophy*, **4**:150–66.

McCloskey, D. (1990), 'Agon and Ag Ec: Styles of Persuasion in Agricultural Economics', *American Journal of Agricultural Economics*, **72**(5):1124–30.

McCloskey, D. (1990), *If You're so Smart: The Narrative of Economic Expertise*, University of Chicago Press, Chicago.

McKenzie, R. (1983), *Limits of Economic Science*, Kluwer, Boston.

Mises, L. (1966), *Human Action* (3rd Edition), Contemporary Books, Chicago 1–69.

Mises, L. (1978), *The Ultimate Foundation of Economic Science: An Essay on Method* (2nd Edition), Universal Press, Kansas City.

Mises, L. (1981), *Epistemological Problems of Economics*, New York University Press, New York

Morgan, T. (1988), 'Theory versus Empiricism in Academic Economics: Update and Comparisons', *Journal of Economic Perspectives*, **2**(4):619–27.

Mueller, D. (1989), *Public Choice II*, Cambridge University Press, Cambridge.

Novick, D. (1954), 'Mathematics: Logic, Quantity and Method', *Review of Economics and Statistics*, **36**(4):357–8.

Oster, R. and R. Wilson (1978), *The Social Insects*, Harvard University Press, Cambridge, MA.

Perry, R. (1912), *Present Philosophical Tendencies, A Critical Survey of Nationalism, Idealism, Pragmatism and Realism Together With a Synopsis of the Philosophy of William James*, Longmans & Green, New York.

Phelby, J. (1988), *Methodology and Economics*, Macmillan, London.

Phelps Brown, Sir E.H. (1972), 'The Underdevelopment of Economics' *Economic Journal*, **82**(March): 1–10.

Pitt, J.C. (ed.) (1981), *Philosophy in Economics*, Reidel Publishing Company, Dordrecht, Holland.

Pope, R. (1978), 'The Expected Utility Hypothesis and Demand-Supply Restrictions', *American Journal of Agricultural Economics*, **60**(4):619–27.

Pope, R. and A. Hallam (1986), 'A Confusion of Agricultural Economists: A Professional Interest Survey and Essay', *American Journal of Agricultural Economics*, **68**(3):572–94.

Popper, K. (1959), *The Logic of Scientific Discovery*, Harper, New York.

Popper, K. (1963/1989), *Conjectures and Refutations* (5th Edition), Routledge, London.

Redman, D. (1991), *Economics and the Philosophy of Science,* Oxford University Press, Oxford.

Ricketts, M. and E. Shoesmith (1992), 'British Economic Opinion: Positive Science or Normative Judgement', *American Economic Review*, **82**(2):210–15.

Robbins, L. (1932), *An Essay on the Nature and Significance of Economic Science*, St. Martin's, London.

Rosenberg, A. (1976), *Microeconomic Laws: A Philosophical Analysis*, University of Pittsburgh Press, Pittsburgh.

Rosenberg, A. (1983), 'If Economics Isn't Science, What is It?' *Philosophical Forum*, **14**:296–314.

Rosenberg, A. (1992), *Economics – Mathematical Politics or the Science of Diminishing Returns*, University of Chicago Press, Chicago.

Rothbard, M. (1976), 'Praxeology: The Methodology of Austrian Economics', in E. Dolan (ed.), *The Foundations of Modern Austrian Economics*, Sheed & Ward, Kansas City.

Roy, S. (1989), *Philosophy of Economics,* Routledge, London.

Samuels, W.J. (1989), *The Methodology of Economic Thought* (2nd Edition), Transaction Books, New Brunswick, New Jersey.

Samuelson, P. (1947/1979), *Foundations of Economic Analysis*, Harvard University Press, Cambridge, MA.

Samuelson, P. (various years), *Economics: An Introductory Analysis*, McGraw-Hill, New York.

Sellars, R. (1966), *Principles of Emergent Realism* (edited by W.P. Warren), Warren H. Green Incorporated, St. Louis.

Senior, N. (1836/1965), *An Outline of the Science of Political Economy*, A.M Kelley, New York.

Shackle, G. (1972), *Epistemics and Economics*, Cambridge University Press, Cambridge.

Shionoya, Y. (1990), 'Instrumentalism in Schumpeter's Economic Methodology', *History of Political Economy,* 22(2):187–222.

Silberberg, E. (1978), *The Structure of Economics: A Mathematical Analysis*, McGraw-Hill, New York.

Sims, C. (1980), 'Macroeconomics and Reality', *Econometrica,* 48(January): 1–48.

Skousen, M. (1991), *Economics on Trial: Lies, Myths and Realities*, Business One Irwin, Homewood, Illinois.

Stewart, I. (1979), *Reasoning and Method in Economics*, McGraw-Hill (UK), London.

Stigler, G. (1983), 'Nobel Lecture: The Process and Progress of Economics', *Journal of Political Economy,* 91(4): 529–45.

Stigler, G. and G. Becker (1977), 'De Gustibus Non Est Disputandum', *American Economic Review,* 62(2):76–90.

Tinbergen, J. (1939), *A Method and Its Application to Investment Activity*, League of Nations, Geneva.

van Frassen, B. (1980), *The Scientific Image*, Oxford University Press, New York.

Ward, B. (1972), *What's Wrong with Economics?* Basic Books, New York.

Weintraub, R. (1985), *General Equilibrium Analysis: Studies in Appraisal*, Cambridge University Press, Cambridge.

White, L. (1977), *The Methodology of the Austrian School Economics*, Ludwig von Mises Institute, Auburn.

Wieser, F. (1927/1967), *Social Economics,* Translated by A.F. Hinrichs, A.M Kelley, New York.

Woo, H. (1986), *What's Wrong with Formalization in Economics?*, Victoria Press, Hong Kong.

Worswick, G. (1972), 'Is Progress in Economic Science Possible?', *Economic Journal,* **82**(March):73–100.

Index